Our Man in Iran

Our Man in Iran

*An American writer travels around
the Islamic Republic
on the edge of war and peace*

by Matthew Stevenson

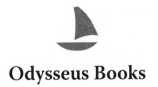

Odysseus Books

OUR MAN IN IRAN
Copyright © 2023 by Matthew Mills Stevenson
ISBN-13: 978-0-9970580-6-2 (paperback)
ISBN-13: 978-0-9970580-7-9 (e-book)

First edition. Manufactured in the United States.
This book was printed on acid-free paper in the United States.
This paper meets the requirements of ANSI/NISO Z39.48-1992

For fulfillment information, address:
Odysseus Books c/o Pathway Book Service,
34 Production Avenue, Keene New Hampshire 03431
Toll free: 1-800-345-6665 Fax: 1-603-357-2073
E-mail: pbs@pathwaybook.com

Other inquiries: Odysseus Books.
Attention: David Wogahn, publisher
publish@partnerpress.org. Tel: 1-877-735-5269

Please visit the book's website: www.odysseusbooks.com
To contact the author on any matter, such as to arrange a
speaking engagement, please use: matthewstevenson@sunrise.ch.
Author website is: www.matthewmstevenson.com

Edited by DEBORAH BANCROFT, CRAIG WHITNEY,
COLE HARROP, and MARTIN DALY.
Cover and book design by NANETTE STEVENSON.
Cartography by MAPPING SOLUTIONS, Anchorage, Alaska.

Library of Congress Cataloging-in-Publication Data
Stevenson, Matthew Mills, 1954–author.
Our Man in Iran / by Matthew Mills Stevenson.
p. cm. (Odysseus Books)
ISBN-13: 978-0-9970580-6-2 (paperback)
1. Stevenson, Matthew Mills, 1954—Travel. 2. Iran. I. Title.

10 9 8 7 6 5 4 3 2 1

This book is dedicated to

*human rights lawyer, book lover, and Napoleonic scholar
who on our honeymoon in 1984 welcomed
my wife and me to Buenos Aires.*

And to my friend

ROB KOCH

who, much like his parents, inspires me.

Contents

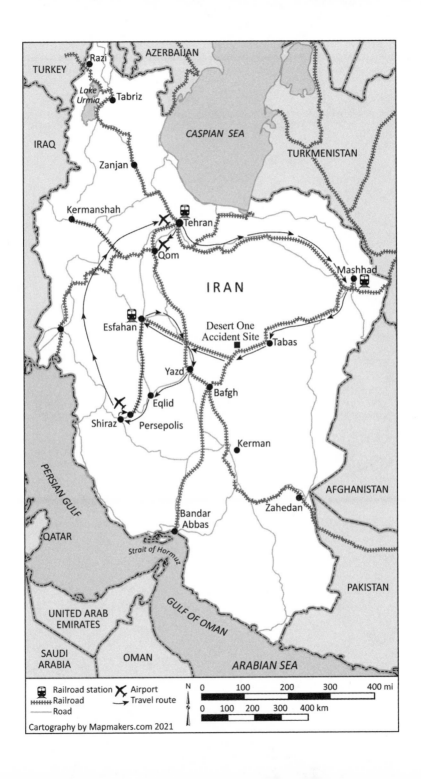

Our Man in Iran

Graduate School Days

MY FIRST THINKING AND READING ABOUT IRAN came in the late 1970s, when I was a graduate student at Columbia University and had to write a paper about U.S. arms sales to the shah. Jimmy Carter was the American President, and he would on occasion appear in the press cozying up to the shah, calling him a bulwark of freedom in a troubled region or praising Iran's support for Israel. Ayatollah Khomeini, if he was in the news at all, was an arm-waving figure in Paris, trying to rally the opposition. I doubt I made mention of him in my paper.

What had sparked my interest in the topic was my reading of Anthony Sampson's *The Arms Bazaar: From Lebanon to Lockheed,* which was published in 1977 and described the nether world of merchants peddling rockets, machine guns, and hand grenades to dodgy regimes, including the shah's. Although the paper has long since vanished, my conclusion was that selling armaments to Iran was a risky business.

Writing the paper, I must also have thought about one day traveling in Iran—my father had been to Tehran once or twice on business, but only briefly. When I left graduate school in the spring of 1978, it was for a full-time job with two weeks' vacation. Whatever thoughts I had about traveling to Iran would have to wait. And then the following year, Ayatollah Khomeini returned from Paris, the shah departed, the hostages were taken, and Iran dropped behind an Islamic iron curtain, outside the realm of travel daydreams.

My only immediate connection to the hostage crisis came in 1982, when I was leaving a magazine job. At my farewell party in a local bar in New York City, my friend George Feifer (the author of many books) showed up in the company of former Iran hostage Barry Rosen. They were collaborating on a book. It was a hectic night for me, but I did speak with Rosen for a few minutes. Even in that brief exchange he struck me as a man of forbearance and compassion, qualities that clearly enabled him to survive the 444-day ordeal. *The Destined Hour* by Barbara and Barry Rosen with George Feifer came out in August 1982, and in it Barry says: "But what was much worse than I imagined, even after a few hours, was being captive." While I kept in touch with George, I had no more contact with Rosen.

In the 1980s and 90s, I continued to collect books and memoirs about Iran (The Strand bookstore in New York had a steady supply), but in the 1980s, Iran was at war with Iraq and a sworn enemy of the United States, making it as unlikely a place to visit as North Korea or Cuba. Iran was also thought to have bankrolled the takers of American hostages in Lebanon and might have funded the radicals that killed some 200 Marines in the barracks at the Lebanon airport.

From Sally Field to *Argo*

IN THE 1990S AND 2000S, I began hearing of small groups or the occasional journalist visiting Iran, but in those days the idea of a trip to Iran sounded like a variation on Jane Fonda's visit to Hanoi during the Vietnam War. Yes, it might be possible, but it could be dangerous, as Americans were unwelcome. Plus, in those days there emerged a genre of films—*Not Without My Daughter* starring Sally Field was just one of them—that preyed on American fears of Iran, which had a habit of detaining visiting Americans, at least those of Iranian origin. In the film, Field has a child with her Iranian husband, a doctor. During a trip home to Tehran, the doctor decides arbitrarily to stay in Iran and raise his daughter behind a burqa. Field thinks otherwise and heads with her daughter to the Turkish border, bringing to the large screen one of the first Islamic chase scenes.

Another Iranian film I saw during these years was 2011's *This Is Not a Film* by Jafar Panahi and Mojtaba Mirtahmasb. I went to an advance screening in Paris at which Costa-Gavras, the Greek/French director and human rights advocate, introduced the film and spoke about intellectual and political freedom. Implausible as it sounds, the Iranian film is shot almost entirely in Panahi's Tehran apartment, where he has been sentenced to house arrest for some of his earlier films and his outspoken stance on human rights.

The only story in the film is Panahi brainstorming with his colleague, Mirtahmasb, about how they could make a film about Panahi's confinement. Little by little, the idea of making a film becomes reality. Panahi speaks to the simple camera, draws production points on the floor, and, when his friend smuggles a better camera into the apartment, records footage of his internal exile. When the film began, I thought it was just another filmmaker's self-indulgent "Song of Myself" but after a while I found myself caught up in the world of Panahi's confinement, anger, and finally enthusiasm for wanting to make a film about political repression and confinement. (Maybe Whitman was right when he wrote: "You shall listen to all sides and filter them from your self.") The film made me admire Panahi for making it, and Costa-Gavras for supporting it, but it didn't make me long to visit Iran. Who would want to visit a country that consigns its filmmakers to house arrest?

The movie that did make me want to go to Iran was *Argo*—not because I liked it, but because I did not. When the film was released in 2012, some of our children went to see it, and came home to report that they had witnessed the truth about the Iranian Revolution. They sounded like the film's posters, which read: "Based on a declassified true story." In case you missed it, *Argo* is the story of the CIA's liberation of six U.S. officials who had eluded capture when, in 1979, students stormed the U.S. embassy compound and took sixty-five hostages. Ben Affleck directed the film, in which he also stars.

From the start, I had my doubts that Hollywood could make anything accurate about the Iran hostage crisis, but when the kids challenged me on my opinion—and it turned out all I had seen was the *Argo* trailer—they rightfully scoffed at my views. (They sounded like my mother, who, when we were growing up and expressing our own opinions about the world, would repeat a comedy line from her childhood: "Wuz you there, Charlie?") Since then, to atone for my Cliff Notes approach to history, I have seen the film twice, read the Canadian memoir on which it is based, and traveled extensively around Iran, in part, I am sure, just to hold my own in dinner-table conversations with my children.

As a CIA recruiting film, *Argo* is fine. As history, it is absurd. In the Hollywood version, the streetwise Affleck plays the brave, good-looking CIA agent Tony Mendez, who sells the fiction that the six embassy officials are actually members of his film crew shooting a science-fiction movie called *Argo* in the rugged wilds of the Iranian desert. Mendez leads them out of Iran on a Swissair plane while Revolutionary Guards chase them down the runway, firing machine guns at the rolling jet.

In reality, the six diplomats left in the pre-dawn darkness at 5:30 a.m. with immigration officials barely looking at their phony documentation and no Guards present to shoot up the runway.

The film also misrepresents the role of the British (who did not turn away the six envoys on the run) and Canadian embassies in the escape, giving the CIA all the film credits. And the Iranians in the film are a cross between made-for-TV mobs and Ayatollah-induced revolutionaries intent on bringing "death to America." *Argo* struck me as on a level with comic book histories—Hollywood could just as easily have sent Batman to get the hostages out, although maybe there was a problem securing the rights. No wonder the U.S. and Iran remained at loggerheads thirty-three years after the hostage crisis. But until I actually went to Tehran, I didn't think my opinion counted for much, especially with my children.

An Iran Trip Primer

THE SIX AMERICAN DIPLOMATS had an easier time leaving revolutionary Iran than I did getting in. Although it is legal for Americans to visit Iran, they are required to travel as part of a group or with a guide at all times.

The first time I looked at going to Iran, I had wanted to take the train from Istanbul and Van, in Turkey, and arrive in Tehran by way of Tabriz. When I applied for a visa, I was told that I would need an escort/guide to meet me after I crossed the Turkish border, although no one could promise me that the guide would be at the Razi rail station when I arrived. Anyway, I dropped the train idea when Iran's Green Revolution in 2012 brought violence into Tehran's streets.

Although I did not want to join a group of package tourists, I did keep browsing Iranian travel web sites until I discovered in 2015 one that had eight-day tours for about $600. The catch was that the travelers went around on the bus and stayed in budget hotels. Intrigued by the backpacker tours, I wrote to the owner of a local travel company, Omid Hosseini, and asked if maybe I could replace the buses on the budget tour with trains? In that way, I would satisfy my visa requirement to be with a guide or tour, and I would be doing it my way, on the train.

Omid wrote back to say that the train was possible, and we spent the next month or so pleasantly e-mailing back and forth about routes, places to visit, and trains to catch. Little

makes me happier than daydreaming about overnight sleepers, and Iran has many long-distance trains between Tehran
and Mashhad, Esfahan, and Shiraz, the principal cities on the
tourist routes.

After a while, Omid and I agreed on a route around
the country, and I filled out another application for a visa,
this time about a month before I was due to leave. For an air
connection from Geneva to Tehran, I picked a $300 ticket
on Ukraine Airlines by way of Kiev (then in the throes of its
Maidan Revolution). "Great," my wife said, "from one war
zone to another. No wonder it was $300."[1]

With everything in place, I hunted around my library
and stacked on my office floor all the books I own about Iran.
Even I was surprised that I had so many. Some were histories of the Persian Wars (with Greece in the fifth century
CE). Others were accounts of the Assassins (a medieval tribe
in Persia—the name referring to the influence of hashish)
and more modern histories of the Kurds, the Great Game
(between Russia and Britain over Persia), the Tehran Conference (which Stalin hosted in 1943), and the coup against
Prime Minister Mohammad Mosaddegh that the CIA pulled
off in 1953. (The coup didn't appear in *Argo*, but it explains
much of the historical anger that Iranians have for Americans.) Finally, I found many books in my library about revolutionary Iran, including the hostage crisis, the so-called

---

1: On January 8, 2020, this same flight, Ukraine International Airlines 752, on its
way from Tehran to Kiev, would come to a fatal end. After taking off from Tehran
Imam Khomeini International Airport, the plane was shot down by a missile fired
(in confusion) by the Iranian Islamic Revolutionary Guards, then in a state of alert
as it was five days after an American drone missile had killed the Iranian general,
Qassim Suleimani. Apparently, the Guards on duty confused the commercial jet
with an incoming missile and fired one of their own.

"twilight war" in and around the Persian Gulf, the civil war in Lebanon (in which Iran played an evil hand), and the war between Iran and Iraq.

At least I would not need to buy more books for my trip, although in the end I took my Kindle with me and during the long train rides (and much to my surprise) I easily logged into Amazon and replenished my traveling library.

A Very Short History of
the Persian Empire

WHILE WAITING TO LEAVE FOR IRAN, I read Stephen Kinzer's
All the Shah's Men, which is an account of the Mosaddegh
coup. I had only seen the story as part of larger histories of
the Cold War; the Kinzer book, bought in 2007 but never
read, looked to me like a readable summary of how the
Americans had overthrown the elected Iranian Government
and installed Reza Pahlavi, who would serve until 1979 as the
Shah of Iran. He also called himself the shah of shahs (the
king of kings), much as his predecessors on the job had called
themselves the Asylum of the Universe, Subduer of Climate,
Arbitrator of His People, Guardian of the Flock, Conqueror
of Lands, and Shadow of God on Earth. If nothing else, the
position came with some nice titles.

Kinzer, a former foreign correspondent for the New
York Times, writes well, although at times the book has the
feel of a long newspaper dispatch. Nevertheless, he summa-
rizes well the dilemmas that faced Iran after World War II,
when Mosaddegh was elected prime minister. He writes:

> Great themes run through Iranian history and shape it to
> this day. One is the continuing and often frustrating effort
> to find a synthesis between Islam, which was imposed on
> the country by Arab conquerors, and the rich heritage
> of pre-Islamic times. Another, fueled by the Shiite Mus-
> lim tradition to which most Iranians now belong, is the

thirst for just leadership, of which they have enjoyed precious little. A third, also sharpened by Shiite beliefs, is a tragic view of life rooted in a sense of martyrdom and communal pain. Finally, Iran has since time immemorial been a target of foreign invaders, victim of a geography that places it astride some of the world's most important trading routes and atop an ocean of oil, and it has struggled to find a way to live with powerful outsiders. All these strains combined in the middle of the twentieth century to produce and then destroy the towering figure of Mohammad Mossadegh.

Kinzer begins his story (after a cursory history of Cyrus, Alexander, and the 2500-year span of the Persian Empire) around 1901, when a British merchant, William Knox D'Arcy, acquired from the Persian shah the "special and exclusive privilege to obtain, exploit, develop, render suitable for trade, carry away and sell natural gas [and] petroleum... for a term of sixty years." Knox D'Arcy was "a London-based financier," and he was wildcatting for a commodity that was new to the Middle East, although he held out hope that Persia might "prove up" some reserves.

Kinzer writes that the deal "pitted, in the words of one historian, 'the Persian trait of openness and assimilation against the Islamic trait of insularity and traditionalism.'" At the turn of the century, oil was largely sought as something that could be sold to the British navy, no doubt the client that Knox D'Arcy had in mind.

In 1907, Russia and Britain signed a treaty partitioning Persia into two spheres of influence—with Moscow dominant in the north, and the English in the south. Kinzer writes: "When the treaty formalizing it came before the British Parliament for ratification, one of the few dissenting members lamented that it left Iran 'lying between life and death, parceled out, almost dismembered, helpless and friendless at our feet.'"

In 1919, as Britain emerged after the war as the dominant power in the Middle East, Lord Curzon, the British foreign secretary, made the case for keeping Persia as an imperial subsidiary, even if nominally it was an independent state. (After the world war, he would say that the Allies had "floated to victory on a wave of oil.") He said:

> If it be asked why we should undertake the task at all, and why Persia should not be left to herself and allowed to rot into picturesque decay, the answer is that her geographical position, the magnitude of our interests in the country, and the future safety of our Eastern Empire render it impossible for us now—just as it would have been impossible for us any time during the last fifty years—to disinherit ourselves from what happens in Persia. Moreover, now that we are about to assume the mandate for Mesopotamia, which will make us coterminous with the western frontiers of Asia, we cannot permit the existence between the frontiers of our Indian Empire and Baluchistan and those of our new protectorate, a hotbed of misrule, enemy intrigue, financial chaos and political disorder.

For its man in Tehran, the British went with Reza Shah Pahlavi—father of the modern-era shah—who in 1925 was allowed, literally, to place the crown on his own head (who else was there to do it?) and ascend the Peacock Throne (although that was Mogul, not Persian).

Reza Shah had been a soldier in a Cossack regiment, although when in power he served British more than Russian

interests. Russia could not object; in the 1920s, it was rejecting Romanov treaties and Stalin was consolidating power
in Moscow. He extended the franchise of the joint venture
(renamed the Anglo-Iranian Oil Company) until 1961. His
model ruler was Kemal Ataturk, in nearby Turkey, who managed to subdue the clerics and modernize the country with
railroads and infrastructure projects.

Nevertheless, the break between the British and the
shah came in the early days of World War II, when Iran (no
longer Persia, which was considered a foreign word; the
shah even returned incorrectly addressed mail) sided with
the Germans to play off the imperial interests of Britain and
Russia. In late 1941, the British delivered the shah his pink
slip ("Sorry, old chap!") and replaced him with his young son,
Mohammad Reza Pahlavi, who would rule until 1979 when
supporters of Ayatollah Khomeini said—to use the Hollywood expression—"Argo fuck yourself."

After the war, Britain viewed Iran as little more than a
filling station for its navy and empire, although both were in
eclipse. Kinzer writes:

> From that moment on, the interests of Britain and the
> Anglo-Persian Oil Company became one and insepara-
> ble. "Mastery itself was the prize of the venture," Chur-
> chill asserted.

Pushing back on imperial hegemony, however, was the
national parliamentarian Mohammad Mossadegh, who was
elected prime minister in 1951, against the better instincts of
the shah. Kinzer writes: "Two central beliefs shaped Mossadegh's political consciousness. The first was a passionate faith
in the rule of law, which made him an enemy of autocracy

and, in particular, of Reza Shah. The second was a conviction that Iranians must rule themselves and not submit to the will of foreigners." Born in 1882, Mossadegh had been educated in Switzerland and worked as a lawyer and parliamentarian until he was called out of retirement and asked to head up the government. He was more the contemporary of the Pahlavi father than of the son.

Mossadegh Throws Out the British

ONCE IN POWER, MOSSADEGH IMMEDIATELY went after the Anglo-Iranian Oil Company. Kinzer quotes a Mossadegh contemporary, saying: "Iran's sovereignty was being undercut by a company that sacrificed Iranian lives for British interests. This is what infuriated him about the government's willingness to compromise—and it is what made him decide unequivocally that AIOC had to go." Three days after his election as prime minister, he cancelled the Anglo-Iranian concession, and nationalized the companies' assets. One statistic that galled him was that in the first fifty years of operation, the company produced 350 million barrels of crude oil, on which Iran earned only £150 million.

Initially, the British took nationalization much harder than did the Americans, as it was a British asset that was taken over. Kinzer writes:

> Truman had received a confidential profile of Mossadegh that reflected the American view of him. It said that he was "supported by the majority of the population" and described him as "witty," "affable," "honest," and "well informed." This could not have been more different from the British view, in which, according to various diplomatic cables and memoranda, Mossadegh was a "wild," "erratic," "eccentric," "crazy," "gangster-like," "fanatical," "absurd," "dictatorial," "demagogic," "inflammatory," "cunning," "slippery," "completely unscrupulous," and "clearly

imbalanced" "wily Oriental" who "looks like a cab horse" and "diffuses a slight reek of opium."

The American view changed after Truman sent roving ambassador Averell Harriman to Tehran in July 1950, and to greet him, Iranian demonstrators filled the street chanting, "Death to Harriman!"

Also on that mission was the American Vernon Walters, later himself something of a coup master for many administrations. He said of Harriman's effort: "It was in a sense a mission that failed, but it was a mission that cast a long shadow ahead on the great problems that the Western world was to have with oil two and a half decades later. These, Dr. Mossadegh was not to live to see, yet in a way their true origin led back to him." The mission might also have tilted the Americans in the direction of a coup.

The British were already there, as Kinzer writes:

> Churchill, who considered Mossadegh "an elderly lunatic bent on wrecking his country and handing it over to the Communists," was willing and even eager to cross that line.... Britain's plan to replace Mossadegh had failed because a mob intervened. Next time... the British must have the mob on their side.

It took another two years for the Americans to succeed in overthrowing Mossadegh. Newly elected President Dwight Eisenhower authorized (or acquiesced to) the CIA's sending Kermit Roosevelt (Teddy's son) to Tehran in summer, 1953, and he plotted with the Iranian military to oust Mossadegh and replace him with Reza Pahlavi as both shah and head of government.

The CIA almost botched the job (another highlight reel that never featured in *Argo*), but by that point Mossadegh had few friends in Tehran. Even the mullahs were willing to see him go, hoping they would have more influence with the shah.

The ousted prime minister said at his trial, which resulted in house arrest: "My only crime is that I nationalized the Iranian oil industry and removed from this land the network of colonialism and the political and economic influence of the greatest empire on earth."

Kinzer quotes an article by Mostafa T. Zahrani, "The Coup That Changed the Middle East: Mossadeq v. The CIA in Retrospect," which appeared in *World Policy Journal* about the American-led putsch: "The 1953 coup and its consequences [were] the starting point for the political alignments in today's Middle East and inner Asia." And Kinzer writes in his own conclusion: "From the seething streets of Tehran and other Islamic capitals to the scenes of terror attacks around the world, Operation Ajax [the code name for the *coup d'état*] has left a haunting and terrible legacy." The students that took over the American embassy might well have been called Mossadegh's Children.

The Curious Case of a Visa in the Night

WHAT GAVE MY FLIGHTS FROM GENEVA to Kiev and Tehran some drama is that I left Switzerland without an Iranian visa. Needless to say, this wasn't my idea, but Omid's. He said he had spoken with the Ministry of Foreign Affairs (MFA) about it, and they told him there had not been time to process the application, and that I could get my visa at the airport on arrival.

It all sounded too casual for my taste—Iran doesn't strike me as a visa-on-arrival kind of place. My choices, however, were simple: I could cancel the trip (losing the $300 for the flights) or I could push ahead and hope for the best with airport immigration. My risk there was that, if turned away at the frontier, I would have to buy a one-way ticket back to Geneva, which could easily cost another $700. Finally, if I postponed the trip, I didn't know when I might have another two weeks to go there.

I spent a few days thinking over the problem and decided to risk getting a visa at the airport. I had come to trust Omid in our e-mail exchanges about train schedules and city options—his thinking often matched mine—and I figured he should know better than I about the MFA. I did recall, however, that during the 1979 hostage crisis, the MFA had held the American *chargé d'affaires* under house arrest. (At least the MFA was always too diplomatic to tell him he was a prisoner.)

The first flight, to Kiev, was half full, but the next flight, to Tehran, had fewer than twenty passengers, as the timing of my travel coincided with a Russian offensive in Eastern Ukraine. (Kiev's more in the west, but the headlines were not helping the airline's business.) We landed around one in the morning, perhaps the last flight of the day. At least the arrival side of Imam Khomeini International Airport was empty, and I easily found the short line of passengers from Kiev in front of the MFA airport visa window.

The two men in front of me looked like Ukrainian arms merchants, and they had been drinking heavily on the flight. Nevertheless, the immigration officer on duty (he was wearing slacks and a shirt, not a military uniform) processed their papers, printed the visa, checked with someone in the back office, and stamped them into the country. The process took ten minutes, and when I stepped up to the window, the officer went through exactly the same steps with my application, making me think I was "in". I could even see the visa sticker with my name on it on his desk. Then he said: "There's a problem. Did you once before apply for a visa?"

His English was good, and I told him about wanting to take the train from Turkey and filling out the visa application, which went nowhere. ("I couldn't find a guide to meet me at Razi...") I began unloading papers from my bag that I had asked Omid to send me, "just in case I have a problem at the airport." He had sent the schedule and verified that I would be with a guide, but the officer on duty seemed unimpressed. I got the feeling that pretty soon I would have to turn around, head back to the departure lounges, and try to bum a ride on a flight to Europe. Maybe *Argo* had been more accurate than I thought?

I didn't plead or argue with the officer (who looked exactly my age), but I didn't leave his desk, either. I just stood there, silently, while he looked at my papers and went again to the back office. Then he sighed out loud over my passport, pasted down the visa, and said: "You know, I shouldn't do this, but welcome to the Islamic Republic of Iran."

I had with me some Swiss chocolates, and I thought of thanking him with a bar, but that seemed over the post-revolutionary line. Instead, I collected my bag, passed through customs (where no one was on duty), and found my cab driver near the exit gate.

Guiding Around Tehran

IT WAS WELL AFTER 2 A.M. WHEN THE TAXI left the airport and drove me to my hotel in Tehran, the Parasto, on a side street in the center of the old downtown, not far from the Russian embassy and the site of the Tehran Conference. (Roosevelt and Churchill, who met Stalin there, skipped meeting with the shah, which tells you what they thought of Iranian sovereignty.)[2]

My room had two twin beds, which suits me well when I am traveling, and on one I unpacked my maps, books, and papers. On the bed closest to the window I fell asleep almost instantly, and slept until 9 a.m., when I ate breakfast and awaited the arrival of my guide, Farshad Mousavi, at 10:30 a.m. Breakfast was juice, cheese, lunch meat, delicious flat bread, hard boiled eggs, and coffee, and I ate the same thing each morning, with pleasure, no matter where I was in the country. Nothing in Iran is better than the morning bread.

I had not known who my guide would be or what he would be like, and I dreaded getting someone fluent only in

---

2: Also on the grounds of what is now the Russian embassy was Atabak Palace, where in 1911 the American Morgan Shuster was stationed, in an effort to bring order to Persia's finances. He was a choir master sent to bring organization to a brothel—he lasted less than a year on the job. In his memoir of the assignment, *The Strangling of Persia,* he wrote: "The destruction of her independence was written down in the book of history at Potsdam in 1910.... Russia is now the sovereign power in Persia. She is the practical and effective ruler of the country. The whole of the country is to-day a satrapy." Shuster left the country in December 1911, much the way an earlier frustrated diplomat in Tehran said to his chauffeur: "Drive me to Europe."

guide-speak—that endless patter about "the early days of the Persian Empire when Cyrus…" I had avoided traveling in China for years when my only choice was going around with a tour group. Omid had said my guide would be "a good one," but he didn't have a name or a profile when I left Geneva, and only when he came through the door did I get Farshad's full name.

My great luck was that Farshad, who was studying for his masters' degree in tourism at the University of Tehran, was in his mid-twenties, had an engaging sense of humor, knew Iran as well as I know Brooklyn, and was game to take me anywhere, discuss anything, and knew, early in our travels, exactly what might interest me (the National Museum) and what would not (expensive meals that take two hours).

Farshad and I spent the next twelve days together, and all I remember now is a general bantering, teasing conversation, many laughs, no arguments or disagreements, and a near-perfect alignment of shared interest in ancient and modern history. (It helped that he was about the same age as my children.) He never said no to my requests or interests (although he did gently guide me in other directions when an idea of mine was stupid), and I loved that he was game for touring whenever—such as one night at 9 p.m. when we rode the subway to south Tehran and saw the tomb of Ayatollah Khomeini. I was always saying things such as, "Where was the house of Mohammad Mossadegh?" and he would tell me, "Well, it's about a hundred kilometers south of here, in Ahmad Abad. The house is there, but I am not sure there is much to see." Although, had I insisted, we would have gone.

Thanks to Farshad, I got into the holy shrine in Mashhad, biked around Esfahan, saw in Tehran where the American hostages were taken, walked around Tehran University, found the Iran-Iraq war museum, and arrived, as I wanted, at Persepolis just as it opened. We ate breakfast at the hotels, lunch on the run, and dinner in neighborhood restaurants. On trains and buses—he knew both systems well—he left me alone to read my books, which I also appreciated.

The Koranic Verses at the Malek Library

AN EXAMPLE OF HIS ENTHUSIASM for travels around Iran came first thing that morning. I mentioned to him that my friend in Geneva, Eugene Schulman, had donated to the Malek Library (opposite the MFA) the first Koran ever printed in English (in 1734). Gene had bought the book in London from a dealer and later met Fatema Soudavar, whose family had endowed the library and were still active in running it.

In my experience, most guides would have nodded at this news and gone on with their program ("if you look above the alcove, you can see a painting that shows the Peacock Throne as it was when the Moguls....").

By contrast, Farshad and I walked to the library, talked our way into the office of a senior librarian, met another member of the staff, and came back two hours later, by which time they had retrieved the book from the rare book room and showed it off to me with pride and pleasure. And we were both fascinated to read the title page, which was printed in two colors:

THE KORAN
COMMONLY CALLED
THE ALCORAN OF MOHAMMED
TRANSLATED INTO ENGLISH IMMEDIATELY FROM THE
ORIGINAL ARABIC; WITH EXPLANATORY NOTES, TAKEN
FROM THE MOFT [MOST] APPROVED COMMENTATORS.

From the library (which was limited to one large floor), we went around the grand bazaar, after first sitting on a park bench to eat sandwiches from a street vendor at the entrance. (All the pushing and shoving in the line next to his cart was a better review than any guidebook endorsement.) Although I wasn't yet in full bargaining mode, I bought a small carpet from a Mr. Pazyryk, who I found myself liking. He served me tea, talked at length about how sanctions had ruined his business (no one could pay with credit cards anymore and few tourists came), and sounded like an Iranian Willy Loman (*"Howard, all I need to set my table is 1,496,557 rials* [fifty dollars] *a week"*).

Never a believer in sanctions (which in my mind only hurt those with no influence on the government in question), I tried and failed to make a connection between a rug merchant in the bazaar and Iran's nuclear ambitions. Before, he had shipped carpets all around the world to his clients; now he could ship on faith or sell for cash to the few tourists wandering the bazaar.

Another thing I learned as Farshad and I walked the bazaar is that Iranians are not a bargaining race. Go to similar bazaar in Tunisia or Egypt, and you will not know a moment's peace. The shopkeepers will follow you, tug on your clothes, quote prices, utter the words "pleez, misters, pleez" about forty times, and then end up by saying, palms turned upward and outstretched, "Okay, okay, best price."

In Tehran, however, at least at the grand bazaar, it is possible to walk through the stalls as one might the Malek

Library. Unless you go over and pick up an object and stand there for a moment with it in your hand, no one will approach you. (In Kinzer's book, he quotes Anthony Eden on the Iranians, as told to Dean Acheson: "They were rug dealers and that's all they were." Clearly Eden had never bought anything in the grand bazaar.) I am not saying that Iranians will not bargain in the market. They will, but they get no pleasure from haggling unlike, say, Moroccans, who live to utter phrases such as "Upon my mother's grave..." when selling a $3 copper cup.

Golestan Gardens and the Shahs' Great Gift Emporium

WE WALKED THROUGH THE PALACE GARDENS of the Goles-tan (think of it as a central campus of the royal family), and then went inside to look at the Museum of Gifts—things given to the shahs over the years.

The palace was the home office of Naser al-Din Shah (and some of his eighty-four wives), a Qajar dynast of the nineteenth century who was a contemporary of Queen Victoria (both in terms of his local importance and when he sat on the throne). Now, in the bazaars anyway, he's a fixture on chess sets and tea pots. Then, he was the first Persian shah to visit Europe, and he signed up the population for various reforms, including the introduction of newspapers, telephones, telegraph, and more universal education.[3]

Either because his reforms went too far or not far enough, Naser al-Din Shah was assassinated in 1886. His last words, like many a regretful tyrant, were: "I will rule you differently if I survive!"

Alas, he did not live to honor the proposed deal, and his heirs—a succession of weaker Qajar shahs, some of whom took up arms against the state—ruled until 1921, when Reza Pahlavi staged his coup. One of the rooms at the Golestan has wax relief figures of the Qajar shahs, including Mozaf-

---

3: He wrote home from Paris: "Even the children speak French."

far ad-Din Shah, who first signed away Persia's oil to Knox D'Arcy.

The tragedy of the Qajar dynasty is that it was attempting to guide Persia into the twentieth century, even toward a constitutional monarchy, but because of the country's geographic location, it always ran afoul of a great power. Away from the crossroads of Russian, British, Indian, and later American imperial designs, Persia and then Iran might have evolved less traumatically.

Mohammad Reza Shah (the last shah) used the Golestan only for state receptions, including his own coronation. His access of power was in the palaces of North Tehran, the section of the city that nestles under the peaks of the Elburz Mountains and above the flatlands of downtown Tehran, where the Golestan is located. It's not unlike Istanbul's Topkapi Palace, where the sultans lived and reigned, sometimes from their harem, which is also on location.

To get around Tehran, Farshad and I rode the bus and subway. With a few changes, we went from the Golestan, first to the University of Tehran and then to the grounds of the former American embassy, where the hostages were taken.

I wanted to see the University because it was students from there who had demonstrated against the shah in 1979, finally overthrowing him. They had also taken over the U.S. embassy, until the government of Ayatollah Khomeini decided that hostages were a useful domestic and international currency and took over the captive business. I read later that the hostage crisis allowed Khomeini to consolidate power internally at a time when his regime was little more than improv theater.

Farshad tried his best to get us into the former American embassy and its anti-American Museum. He talked to the guards stationed at the gate; they told him the embassy was, at that moment, given over to training sessions for the Revolutionary Guard, who took title to the complex after the crisis ended in 1981. (The hostages were released on the same day Ronald Reagan took over the presidency from Jimmy Carter. The Iranians waited until Carter was out of office, as a parting "Argo fuck yourself" to the outgoing president.) Some days, yes, the guard on duty said to Farshad, it was possible to see inside the embassy, but not today.

Instead we walked around the grounds and took pictures, which didn't seem to bother anybody. Before taking any pictures, I would ask Farshad: "Is this okay?" He usually said yes.

On the walls outside was the only anti-American image I saw on the entire trip: a graffiti picture of the Statue of Liberty standing in front of an American flag, except instead of Lady Liberty under the crown, the face in the artwork is a skull, the new colossus of death.

The Real Story of *Argo*

Even if I had been allowed into the former embassy, I would not have learned much more about the hostages than if I watched another episode of *Argo*. Political museums around Iran (there's one across the street from the embassy) tend to use the word "martyr" in most captions, and the theme in many of the exhibits is the death struggle that went on, after 1979, between the revolutionaries (the good guys) and the counter-revolutionaries (the shah supporters and various bad guys).

To understand more about the hostage crisis, I had downloaded onto my Kindle, and read that evening back in the hotel, Robin A. Wright's *Our Man in Tehran: The True Story Behind the Secret Mission to Save Six Americans during the Iran Hostage Crisis & the Foreign* [Canadian] *Ambassador Who Worked with the CIA to Bring Them Home.*

The book was published two years before *Argo* came out, and it would have been among the texts that the producers used to figure out the story. Unfortunately, Canadian Ambassador Kenneth D. Taylor's story of the hostage crisis and Affleck's are at variance. In the book, for example, it's the hostages, not the fearless agents of the CIA, who vote on leaving the country under the cover of a film-location mission. Another omission in the movie is the extent to which Taylor collaborated with the CIA during the entire crisis, not just over the six hostages. Wright says:

And herein lies the greatest irony of all. For while the Canadian ambassador found himself the object of adulation for his role in the exfiltration of the houseguests, he was silent about the operational details of the mission, and also about his—and Jim Edward's—far more "heroic" intelligence-gathering work on behalf of the CIA, the State Department, the Carter White House and the Pentagon. Spying on the militants who had imprisoned the hostages at the U.S. embassy and the Iranian foreign ministry is one of the riskiest assignments known to have been given to a Canadian diplomat in peacetime. Yet Taylor has never mentioned it publicly. He was thus accused of taking too much credit for an operation he well knew was a broad collaborative effort, and was given none at all for a second, far more dangerous mission, one that was his and Edward's alone.

Before reading the book, I had heard Taylor give a speech that was rebroadcast on YouTube, in which he, very diplomatically, explains to the audience how *Argo* had omitted important elements of the story. His speech and the book, however, tell the same story, which (if you ask me) is that the CIA missed the coming of the Iranian Revolution and, after it happened, was flat-footed in Tehran to the extent that it had few, if any, Persian-speaking agents in the county and needed Taylor to act as the *de facto* station chief.

If the Ken Taylor story had been made into a movie instead of *Argo*, it could have been both exciting and factually accurate, although maybe not a Hollywood hit. (Think of a Canadian documentary, with French subtitles.)

* * *

In 1977, young Ambassador Taylor arrived in Tehran. His mission was to promote Canadian exports into the local market, as well as to talk up Canadian companies among Iranian investors. His first impressions of Tehran are of its random chaos. He quotes an unnamed Canadian journalist who says: "Tehran is often described as one huge traffic jam, but it's far worse than that—it's more like one vast head-on collision."

He presented his credentials to the shah in a ceremony at the Niavaran Palace, where Farshad and I walked around one afternoon. It's a collection of large houses and buildings, like the campus of a private university. Wright observes: "The Niavaran Palace complex in the Shemiranat district of North Tehran was the permanent home of the shah and his entourage, the seat of Western power in the Middle East and the nerve centre of one of the most security-obsessed regimes in the world." Early in his stay, Taylor was told: "The Shah's father was a dictator pretending to be a nice man. The Shah himself is a nice man pretending to be a dictator."

Taylor's arrival in Tehran coincided with Jimmy Carter's presidency and the President's infatuation with the shah and his wife. (Wright quotes well-worn Carter praise of the shah's Iran: "Iran, because of the great leadership of the shah," said Carter, "is an island of stability in one of the more troubled parts of the world. This is a great tribute to you, your majesty, and to your leadership, and to the respect and admiration and love which your people give to you.") The two leaders had met in the White House and liked each other, which led to Iran being given something of a hall pass on human rights, which otherwise defined Carter's foreign policy. Wright concludes:

It was not long before the grim consequences of Carter's personal diplomacy were resonating in the jails of Tehran. The moment the shah returned home from Washington, he returned to his hard-line stand against political dissidence, freeing SAVAK [the Iranian secret police] to undertake the worst repression Iran had seen in a year.... Brzezinski would later say that Carter's mixed messages to the shah at this critical juncture were the undoing of his Iran policy and ultimately of his presidency.

On the ground in Tehran, Taylor learned quickly that there is the international shah—the one who skies in St. Moritz and speaks to Carter in perfect English—and the domestic shah, who like so many of his predecessors lives in paranoia about the shadowy opposition. Wright describes the repression infrastructure:

By 1977, when Ken Taylor arrived in Tehran, SAVAK had approximately 5,300 employees, 55,000 informers and an annual budget of $225 million.... In 1980, the Pakistani journalist Eqbal Ahmed estimated that the number of Iranians killed under torture or execution since the 1953 coup totaled 125,000. "Iranians believe it was 150,000 or more," wrote Ahmed, "but God only knows. Iran's best poets died under torture. Iran's finest writers lived in prisons."

Nor, when the street demonstrations grew against the shah, was the United States just another power on the horizon; it was the shah's closest ally and supplier of military hardware and advisers. Wright: "With some 54,000 Americans in Iran by that time—2,000 of them posted to the U.S.

embassy in Tehran and another 10,000 working as military advisers—it was entirely plausible to many ordinary Iranians that their country was precisely what the shah's enemies said it was: a vast network of American spies who collaborated with SAVAK and propped up the lackey shah." Pretty soon, in the streets, the chants of "Death to Carter!" mixed easily with those crying "Death to the shah!"

Despite all the military assets at his disposal, the shah didn't have enough of a dictator's love of blood to shoot down Iranians in the street. He did, on several occasions, allow SAVAK to have its head, notably on so-called Black Friday, when "hundreds, perhaps thousands" were killed, according to Wright and Taylor.

The shah resisted imposing martial law and eventually decided on exile in Egypt as opposed to a full-scale crackdown on the opposition. In early 1979, he flew his own presidential plane (a chase plane had loyal retainers and the family's luggage) out of the country. He would never return.

Carter's loyalty to the shah, after he was forced out of Tehran and then fell ill with cancer, weakened his resolve to distance himself from the deposed king of kings, and he later allowed the shah to travel to New York hospital for treatment. To Iranians in the streets, allowing the shah into the United States was an act of betrayal.

America Held Hostage in 1979

JUST AFTER AYATOLLAH KHOMEINI RETURNED TO TEHRAN, in February 1979, there was a brief takeover of the American embassy—known among the Americans as the Valentine's Day Open House—which local police quickly resolved. Nevertheless, sitting in the center of Tehran, behind old brick walls and metal gates, the sprawling embassy complex remained a ripe target for street demonstrators.

In November 1979, Tehran University students (some with bolt cutters hidden under their dresses) stormed the grounds and took sixty-six hostages (thirteen hostages, women and minorities, would later be released). Wright and Taylor say: "The students arrived at the embassy's front gates as planned at about 9:50 a.m. Iranian police standing post at the entrance did nothing to impede them—a lapse of security that the Americans immediately recognized as collusion."

Later, when Ayatollah Khomeini saw the street value of an American hostage—his son was often at the embassy in the early days, talking to the kidnappers—he replaced the freelance captors with more professional terrorists, some from the Revolutionary Guards but others from Lebanon, where they had trained with the Palestinian Liberation Organization, outside Beirut. These guards changed the tenor of the captivity. As Wright quotes, someone on the inside said: "Their knowledge of interrogation techniques certainly goes beyond being a freshman in university."

At first, the Carter administration thought the hostage situation would quickly pass, as it had in February. Wright and Taylor describe the preoccupation that night in Washington, D.C., not with the embassy takeover but with a speech by potential presidential rival, Senator Edward Kennedy.

When it became clear that the crisis would not pass quickly, the U.S. lacked the personnel on the ground in Tehran to explain who was in charge of the government, who might secure the release of the hostages, or even where and how they were being held.

In *Argo*, Ben Affleck is the self-confident, Hollywood CIA agent with lots of contacts locally to rent cars, hire drivers, and care for the six hostages. Taylor, however, says: "Other than Bob [a Cold War era spy infiltrated in Iran during the crisis], the CIA had no human intelligence of its own in Tehran prior to March 1980." That negligence meant Ambassador Taylor had to operate in their stead, as Wright describes:

> Ambassador Taylor served as the de facto CIA station chief in the weeks before Bob's arrival. Louis Delvoie's ability to insulate Taylor from interference from Langley was critical to the ambassador's ability to function in this new role, allowing him to make command-level decisions based on his understanding of what was happening on the ground in Tehran.

The conclusions in *Our Man in Tehran* are more damning; it contains this passage:

> "If they were a proper intelligence agency," said Edward, "I don't believe that the embassy would have been taken

over—not once but twice—because in the intelligence community this is what it is all about. They are supposed to know what the activities are that are going on in the country. And to actually have all their agents captured in front of the facility at one time and have no knowledge whatsoever of the potential threat. I think that is asinine!" How the CIA reacted to Edward's critique is not known.

Real-life CIA agent Tony Mendez did exfiltrate the six envoys, who had been hiding at various locations in Tehran (not all together at Taylor's house as shown in the movie). However, according to Taylor's account of the history, the CIA cover story was not as elaborate as the one depicted in the movie. Taylor's wife purchased three separate sets of airline tickets out of Iran, just in case of a problem with the Swissair flight (there was none).

Nor were the six hassled at Mehrabad Airport, but who wants to end a Hollywood film with a group of travelers, in the pre-dawn darkness, sitting listlessly in plastic airport chairs, drinking coffee or browsing in gift shops. The idea had been to keep the six in seclusion until the hostage crisis was over, but a Montreal newspaper broke the story the day after they were flown to Zurich, which strained Canadian relations with the revolutionary government.

When the six were out, Taylor got a cryptic phone message, "The party's over; the guests have gone home." The remaining fifty-three Americans would party on for another year and, after the Carter administration botched the rescue attempt, find themselves held hostage, sometimes blindfolded, in apartments all over Tehran.

The Tomb of the Ayatollah

STILL GETTING OVER JET LAG IN TEHRAN, I ate dinner early that night. Then, wanting to know more about Ayatollah Khomeini and what drove him to power, I suggested to Farshad that we go to the south of the city (a more working-class district) to see the ayatollah's tomb. He was game, as always, and led me south on the metro for about a half hour to the Shahed stop, from which it was a ten-minute walk through a parking lot to the complex that houses the ayatollah's tomb.

Because much of the mausoleum is a work in progress—apparently the budget for the project exceeded $2 billion—Farshad and I got lost looking for the entrance, and we errantly walked a long way around the job site, trying to find a way in. Because it was evening, not many pilgrims were there, so there was no one to ask for directions. Finally, we found a watchman on the north side; he sent us back to a tunnel not far from the metro stop.

When it is finished, the shrine to Imam Khomeini will supposedly rival those at Mashhad, Qom, and perhaps Najaf. For the moment, it is a random collection of shrines, mosques, and related buildings that glow in the dark. (From a distance I first thought it was an oil refinery.) The imam's tomb, however, has been relegated to the basement of one shrine. We walked a long way through a subterranean hallway, much of it lined with green carpeting (even on the walls), and then checked our shoes at a kiosk near the entrance. I asked Farshad if it was acceptable for a non-believer to visit the tomb, and he said it was fine. (I learned over the next ten days that the Shia religion, despite its reputation for fanaticism, is extremely tolerant of visitors to its holy sites, and that once inside, informality reigns.)

I had expected the tomb of the ayatollah to be under the dome of an exquisite mosque. Instead, it was fenced off behind a silver grill in an underground room. A lot of the lighting was neon, so the feeling was that of a subterranean garage.

The tomb is open 24/7, but because of the late hour only a few people were pressed up against the grill work. Some were tucking currency bills into small openings in the plastic behind the frame, others were praying on the Persian carpets that surround the tomb.

Farshad and I sat on the rugs and, in a whisper, he told me about Khomeini's career in what might be called religious politics. I got to like these mosque and shrine conversations that we had all over Iran. It felt like chatting in a café, except that we were sitting Indian style on lush carpeting. Later, when I wanted to remember additional details about Khomeini's life, I went to James Buchan's history of the Revolution, *Days of God*, although Farshad knew well the facts of the imam's long and eventful life.

Ayatollah Khomeini
Comes Back to Power

THE MAN KNOWN TO THE WORLD as Ayatollah Khomeini was born in 1902 as Sayyid Ruhollah Mostafavi Musavi and grew up in the town of Khomeyn. His father was murdered when he was three. His mother and extended family (in which there were prominent clerics) saw to both his education and religious training, and at young age he showed a facility with Islamic doctrines.

At age 19, Khomeini moved to Qom, the shrine city 150 kilometers south of Tehran, and he stayed there until the 1960s, when the shah forced him into exile, first in Najaf, in Iraq, and later in Paris. Khomeini's life was one of study and teaching, and he studied everything from Islamic law to Greek philosophy, but where he made his mark, according to Buchan, is with his understanding of Sufi mystics. Buchan writes: "He reasoned in old-fashioned syllogisms, which are often quite vacuous, used violent and vulgar language, and was careless in matters of fact. As a mystic, some Iranians say, he was beyond compare."

While he was teaching, writing, and studying in Qom, Khomeini took on occasional political roles, speaking against the rule of the Pahlavi (father and son). In the 1940s and 50s, despite Khomeini's growing reputation for his Islamic think-ing, he was limited in what role he could play politically; the shah paid only lip service to the clerics, especially when

Western aid began pouring into the country after the 1953 *coup d'état.*

In 1963, Khomeini rallied clerical opposition across Iran to the shah's so-called White Revolution, a series of reforms that were to modernize Iran (and, Khomeini felt, weaken clerical influence). The shah, for example, wanted universal education, including for women, and was open to non-Muslims holding political office—all things anathema to Khomeini.

Among the hot button issues for Khomeini in this time were the so-called Capitulations—the legal waiver that Reza Shah (the father) gave to foreigners, making them exempt from Iranian law. The Americans, in particular, did not want their nationals subject to local laws, even in cases of murder.

Finally, Khomeini had found a good safe menace—the United States—to go with his doctrinal eloquence and outrage. Buchan writes: "By 1964, he was the undisputed champion not just of the seminary but of the clergy in general, of Iranian customs and the Constitution, and the scourge of the monarchy, Israel, and the United States." The shah took his pronouncements personally and ordered Khomeini into exile.

Together with his son, the ayatollah flew to Baghdad, where no one met them at the airport. They waited in the terminal for a while, as Buchan writes, after which "they took a taxi to the Shia shrine of Kazemain, in the western suburbs of the city. Khomeini haggled over the fare. They roomed in a pilgrims' boardinghouse."

Khomeini would stay thirteen years in Najaf, continuing his teaching and writing, but increasingly positioning himself as a leader in the political opposition to the shah. His lectures on the importance of Islamic law (Sharia) were recorded on cassette tapes and circulated in Iran, although the 1960s were a time of prosperity for the shah and his policies, and the ayatollah sounded like a tired old man, shouting into the void.

Khomeini failed to acquire a following in Iraq, and mostly spoke to Iranians making the pilgrimage to Najaf, a holy city within the Shia religion. There he might have died a shrill old man, but in 1978, the shah decided to press Iraq again to deport the ayatollah, and this time he was accepted in France.

From media obscurity in Najaf, Khomeini flew to a Paris suburb, Neauphle-le-Chateau (Buchan: "a sort of Qom translated to the frosty Ile-de-France"), where he installed himself on carpets under an apple tree and had instant access to the world's press whenever he denounced the shah and the Americans. He said, for example: "If Mr. Carter wishes to display his good will, ensure calm, and prevent bloodshed, he should take the shah away." Clearly, later on, he changed his mind.[4]

After Black Friday in 1978, the shah was caught in a no-man's land. He did not want to go forward toward a military government, nor could he go back to his earlier Persian paternalism. He decided that his only choice was a flight to exile. (In his mountain of luggage, he carried a small box of Iranian soil that stayed with him until the end.) In the other

---

4: Once in Paris, I rode my bicycle to Neauphle-le-Chateau, to see if I could find the house where Khomeini had lived in exile. I had no luck finding the house until I stopped a mailman, and he gave me directions to where the imam had held his open-air court. As it turned out, the celebrated apple tree, under which Khomeini spent many afternoons on Persian carpets receiving guests, was across the street from the house where he lived. And next door to the revolutionary suburban house lived the mailman's sister, who apparently thought the ayatollah was an excellent neighbor, although I am not sure that included lending her cups of sugar or popping around to fix her broken lawnmower.

direction, on a chartered Air France Boeing 747 filled with prime-time journalists, came the returning Ayatollah Khomeini who was met, at the airport and on nearby streets, by crowds that measured in the thousands, all delirious with joy.

A sense that Khomeini was returning to settle scores, not to lead a homecoming parade, could be glimpsed in a short, unemotional answer that he gave to a Peter Jennings' question on the flight to Tehran. Jennings asked him how he felt about returning to his homeland. Khomeini, who did not speak English and spoke through an interpreter, said flatly: "Nothing" or perhaps "Nothing at all." It was the first inkling some had that the returning ayatollah was man of few sentiments.

Khomeini set himself up in a religious school in south Tehran and began running the government that the shah had left behind. On the form that the new government would take, he said: "I will decide the government. To oppose it is to deny God as well as the will of the people." He ordered the execution (without due process) of many from the shah's government or in the potential opposition to Sharia law. He said, as quoted in Buchan: "There can be no objection to the trial of these people. They are criminals and it is known that they are criminals. All this about a lawyer being present, and a right to appeal. These are not people charged with crimes. They are criminals."

For a brief time, there was the feeling that the ayatollah might work alongside a liberal democratic civil administration, but the few governments that formed after the ayatollah returned were short-lived affairs. Government was the province of one man, although around him he tolerated the presence of the Revolutionary Guards—his faithful henchmen—who moved into the shah's repressive prisons without even changing the locks.

The ayatollah held on to the hostages to consolidate his domestic position, but he reached a settlement on their release after Iraq invaded Iran in autumn 1980 and Khomeini's government needed access to Western arms dealers. Ideology has its limits.

Settling Accounts After the Hostage Crisis

THE DEAL KHOMEINI CUT to release the captives, in exchange for unfreezing Iran's bank accounts, is another detail that, had *Argo* decided to go there, would have shed new light on the well-worn theme of America-the-victim in the hostage crisis (whom only the CIA can save from shame).

Buchan has an illustrative passage about how American banks, not Revolutionary Guards, were the winners in the hostage exchange. He writes:

> Some $7.95 billion in gold bullion and securities was to pass to an escrow account, Dollar Account One, at the Bank of England. Of that, $3.67 billion would be placed at the New York Federal Reserve to cover Iran's liabilities to U.S. banks and corporations on pre-revolutionary loans and contracts. A further $1.41 billion of Iranian money would fund an international tribunal for the arbitration of commercial claims and counterclaims. The clerical government, as innocent in matters of money as Reza Pahlavi in 1933 and Mossadeq in 1952, would receive in cash just $2.88 billion. It was now clear who was hostage and who hostage-taker.

The war with Iraq brought World War I trenches to the rivers and estuaries that defined the border between Iran and Iraq. After initial Iraqi gains, the Iranians managed to hold their lines. By 1982, they had expelled Iraq from Iranian territory, including some oil-rich lands at the mouth of the Persian Gulf. Iraq offered a ceasefire, in effect *status quo ante*. Ayatollah Khomeini rejected the ceasefire offer and decided to pursue the war into Iraq. Buchan writes: "With that decision, he transformed victory into defeat."

In the last six years of the barbaric fighting, Iran would send waves of school children forward to clear minefields; on its side, Iraq fought with chemical weapons. Buchan writes: "In the eight years of war, Iran by its own computation had lost 123,220 men dead in action, with a further 60,711 missing in action (including deserters and prisoners of war), which was later increased to 72,753." Tehran has a memorial museum to the war; when we went there, Farshad talked about how his father had fought at the desperate front.

The Iran-Iraq war ended in 1988, and a year later Ayatollah Khomeini died. At his funeral, such were the crowds that swarmed around his coffin in the streets that part of his cortege was torn apart, and only the lucky intervention of security guards kept the ayatollah's body from being scattered to the divine winds. His self-appointed successor, Ayatollah Ali Khamenei, has remained the Supreme Leader since 1989.

About Khomeini's turbulent life, Buchan says that "his mystical writings pass over our heads and his political statements, with their exaggerations and inaccuracies, beneath our notice. We wonder how, precisely, he explained to God the spots of blood on his robe and turban and the boys he left behind at Fish Lake," (referring to the siege of Basra at the end of war, during which the Iranians may have suffered 65,000 casualties in less than two months of fighting to break the Iraqi lines).

The Shah's Island of Stability

THE NEXT DAY, FARSHAD AND I WENT NORTH after breakfast and visited North Tehran, including Niavaran Palace, where Mohammad Shah (the last one) lived until he fled the country in January 1979.

Surrounded by a supporting cast of outbuildings, including the Sahebqraniyeh Palace from the time of Naser al-Din Shah, the Niavaran complex has the feel of a state college campus, on which tall trees shade the buildings. When I was there, it was February, and the last of the winter's snow was melting on the sidewalks. (North Tehran is at the same altitude as most alpine ski resorts.)

The shah's 1960s palace, down a long tree-lined path, is a large, rectangular building faced with marble. To me, it looked more like the central bank of Romania than anyone's house. Inside the front door is a large, barren reception hall—I imagined Ambassador Ken Taylor presenting his credentials here—where, in good days, the shah ran the public side of his government, and where, in the last days, he prepared to take his final step "from the sublime to the ridiculous" (which is the Napoleonic phrase that Empress Eugenie chose to recall in 1870, when she herself was fleeing a mob at the Tuileries).[5]

5: Her full quote was: "There is no country in the world where the step from the sublime to the ridiculous is as short as in France." Until that moment she was empress of France. When she stepped away from her royal palace, she was disguised as a char woman.

Walking around Niavaran, I was reminded of a book that I read prior to my trip, entitled *The Shah's Last Ride* by William Shawcross, about his exile that was played out in Egypt, the United States, Mexico, the Bahamas, and Panama, before he died back in Egypt. The trip into exile began on helicopters that landed at Niavaran to pick up the Pahlavis and their luggage (reports vary on the number of suitcases they carried, but Shawcross counts the pieces at 386). It ended in Aswan, in a palace that the Egyptian President, Anwar Sadat, lent to the homeless shah, perhaps at the cost of his own life. (Sadat had cozied up to Jimmy Carter and Israel at Camp David in 1979 and taken in the shah in 1979–80. Islamic holy warriors killed him, on parade, in 1981.)

I was at *Harper's Magazine* in the late 1970s when the shah was on the road and front-page news. As an editor, I worked on several of Shawcross's pieces for the magazine, including one about Henry Kissinger and the bombings in Cambodia. Later in the 1980s, when his book about the shah was published, I bought a copy but held off reading it after one review said it was an apologia for the shah. Only when I read the book in 2014 did I realize that Shawcross had written one of the best biographies of the shah—not in any way an apologia.

Mohammad Shah ended his life as if crewing on the Flying Dutchman (no one wanted him in their country), but his life reads as a cautionary tale on the efficacy of great power politics.

Mohammad Reza Shah was born in 1919 in Tehran. At the Golestan Palace, there is a picture of him as a small boy, fully dressed in a military uniform, walking beside his father during his 1925 coronation. He had his education in Tehran (probably from palace tutors), but then attended high school at Le Rosey in Switzerland, on the lake near Geneva. There he found a degree of freedom from his domineering (Cossack-trained) father, became fluent in several languages including English and French, and acquired a taste for womanizing, skiing, and the continental lifestyle. He joined the Iranian army in 1938, and a year later his father arranged his marriage to Princess Fawzia, who bore him a daughter but who never stood between Mohammad and a good European night club.

After the British overthrew his father as shah in 1941, Mohammad Reza toed the British line through World War II, allowing supplies to travel (on his father's trans-Iranian rail line) from the Persian Gulf to Russia, which was desperate for Allied aid. Left to his own devices in the 1950s, he would not have nationalized Anglo-Iranian Oil, as did Mohammad Mossadegh, but he went along with his prime minister, feeling he had no choice in the matter. (His father, once a sergeant in a Cossack regiment, would have dealt differently with dissent than did his son, who came of age in Maxim's of Paris.)

The 1953 coup against Mossadegh, however, left the shah as head of government and state. Shawcross quotes him as saying to Kermit Roosevelt: "I owe my throne to God, my people—and you."

In the late 1950s and 60s, the shah pushed Iran on a course of modernization, from which he hoped it would emerge as a secular state that could dominate the crossroads of the Middle East, both economically and culturally. In October 1971, the shah invited the world's political and show-business elite to Persepolis, where he celebrated the 2,500th anniversary of the Persian Empire with chefs flown in from Paris and caviar served with ice-cream scoopers. He asserted his independence from his American handlers when in 1973 he supported both the OPEC oil boycott and the subsequent boost in petroleum prices.

Despite the occasional fits of independence, the shah remained Washington's man. From Eisenhower to Nixon (John F. Kennedy had some doubts about him) the U.S. saw Iran as its regional subsidiary, there to do America's bidding in an increasingly unstable part of the world and to act as a bulwark against Russian encroachment to the south.

Despite ruling with an iron fist, the shah managed to convince Jimmy Carter that he was one of the good guys, such that, on their first New Year's Eve in office, the Carters flew to Tehran to celebrate with their good new friends, the Pahlavis. (That's when Carter delivered his "island of stability" toast, in Niavaran Palace.)

Ironically, in view of the current tensions over Iran's nuclear ambitions, it was the Americans in the 1970s who encouraged the shah to acquire atomic technology, if only for peaceful purposes. (The shah had no reason to turn down such a generous gift.) Another gift that the Nixon administration gave to the shah was that he would be the one, not the Pentagon, to decide which weapon systems Iran would purchase.

Trained as a pilot, the shah spent his evenings leafing through armament magazines as if through a L.L. Bean catalogue, and he sent off his orders from a small office in a palace next door to Niavaran (his so-called working study). In the late 1970s, the Iranian army had some of the latest weapon systems in the world, thanks to American generosity. This unconditional largesse explains, too, how it came to pass that, on his first trip to Esfahan, Ambassador Ken Taylor saw rows of helicopters sitting in an empty field.[6]

Shawcross describes the atmosphere of Iran during its go-go years, when the shah's family considered "Iran a business, not a country":

> In the 1970s, the whole country became a wonderland for businessmen and -women. Kickbacks, bribes, agents' fees, secret understandings between princes and PR men, princesses and CIA agents, Samsonite briefcases packed with hundred-dollar bills hand-carried on executive jets, companies with PO box addresses in the Caribbean and Liechtenstein, secret orders and counterorders conveyed in private meetings with the shah — this was the stuff of which business was made from 1973 onwards....
>
> In the mid-seventies, Teheran became one of the nastier capitals of a world in which capital cities were being degraded faster than most assets. Cars were imported by the tens of thousands; traffic jammed to a halt. Power cuts were frequent. Tempers became uncontrollable. Envy was everywhere. Disappointment was the norm.

No wonder the cassette recordings of the ayatollah's lectures—sent in from Najaf and Paris—began to draw such a following.

Shawcross captures well the sense of disbelief and isolation that engulfed the shah and his family at the end. He

---

6: A friend of Taylor's recalled of the trip: "We landed at Isfahan airport, and on the other side of the airport was a huge field—it looked like a square mile—of military helicopters that the shah had bought from the U.S. Helicopters as far as the eye could see. For what? You could see there the conspicuous waste. What was he defending himself against?"

describes a lunch that British diplomat Sir Brian Urquhart attended at Niavaran: "Urquhart found the shah highly opinionated and unable to have an argument—the meeting was a monologue." Later he met with Princess Ashraf, the shah's sister and a power behind the throne (with much more of her father's Cossack tenacity than the son inherited). Shawcross writes: "Urquhart found the food excellent, the conversation non-existent. 'There was an atmosphere of overwhelming nouveau-riche, meretricious chi-chi and sycophancy.... There was an overheated, overstuffed atmosphere in these super-deluxe mini palaces in the imperial compound which left one gasping for air.'"

In exile, the shah's imperial entourage moves around with the air of a touring circus. He's playing golf in Morocco when Khomeini executes many of the shah's senior officers and government officials. In the Bahamas, their luggage will not fit into the beach house they have rented (at extortionate prices), so it is secured under tarpaulin sheets that allow in the rain. The Panamanians are equally happy to overcharge for parking the shah's wagon train, despite packing him off to a rundown villa on an island off the south coast.

Even in New York, where the shah is treated for his cancer, he has the air of the man who came for dinner. The Rockefellers and Henry Kissinger have pushed the Carter government to admit him for treatment (one reason the students overran the embassy), but at New York hospital he's moved between buildings through a dimly lit basement piled with garbage, to keep him away from the inquiring press. Once the shah has fled from Iran and the ayatollah is in power, the United States no longer needs him, but there are no halfway houses for discarded dictators.

Back on the ground in Tehran, with its diplomats held hostage, the Americans know no more about the situation locally than they did when the shah was inviting them to the sound-and-light show at Persepolis. Until March 1980, as Ken Taylor remarked, the CIA had no Persian-speaking asset in Tehran. Nor did the Carter administration have a clue to who might be in charge, aside from the ayatollah. According to Taylor, Jimmy Carter dispatched former attorney general Ramsey Clark and former foreign-service officer William Miller "on a secret mission to Tehran to make direct contact with Khomeini."

From his human rights work, Clark had contacts among Iranian nationalists who had suffered under the shah. The ayatollah, however, had no interest in meeting Clark (by then a Greenwich Village lawyer), and their plane got no closer to Tehran than Ankara. Clark later did himself no favors with anyone, when he came to Tehran to participate in a "Crimes of America" conference.

Of diplomatic contacts with the opposition, the United States had few. Shawcross writes about the last U.S. ambassador to Iran, William Sullivan, who left in 1979 before the hostages were taken, when only a skeleton staff of eighty persons remained. He writes that when Sullivan "asked his staff to give him more information on the nature of Shiite beliefs and ambitions, he had found that there was almost no contact between the mullahs and the embassy. No one had thought they mattered."

Sullivan had little time for the President's National Security Advisor, Zbigniew Brzezinski. During a street demonstration in February, Sullivan took a phone call from Under Secretary of State David D. Newsom, who called from the White House Situation Room. Shawcross describes this scene:

> Newson began: "The National Security Advisor has asked for your view of the possibility of a *coup d'état* by the Iranian military to take over from the Bakhtiar government, which is clearly faltering." [Brzezinski hoped throughout the crisis that Kermit Roosevelt might return to the scene and set things right.]
>
> Sullivan replied: "Tell Brzezinski to fuck off."
>
> Newson responded: "That's not a very helpful comment."
>
> Sullivan asked: "You want it translated into Polish?" and hung up.

No wonder American diplomacy in Iran was never on the same page.

The Night Train to Mashhad

WE WERE TAKING THE OVERNIGHT TRAIN from Tehran to Mashhad, a city in the east, near the border with Afghanistan. In working out the schedule with Omid, I had picked Mashhad because it offered one of the longest train journeys in Iran. Based on my reading, I had thought the holy shrine was off-limits to foreigners. Nevertheless, as we waited in Tehran for the overnight train to be called, Farshad said he thought it would be "no problem" for me to get inside the holy sites. He could not promise anything, he said, but most likely I would be fine going inside the religious complex.

The main Tehran railroad station glowed in the dark when we arrived outside in a taxi. On one side of the soaring windows around the front stood a portrait of Ayatollah Khomeini. On the other side was Ayatollah Khamanei, but in the soft lighting and spring air, they looked more like welcoming railroad officials (*"Route of the Empire Builder"*) than supreme leaders of darkness. Inside, there were a few gift stalls and seats for waiting passengers. I bought water to drink and drifted around the kiosks, and then we joined the line of passengers heading toward their compartments.

Iranian train passengers—at least, the ones heading to Mashhad that night—are well mannered and dressed impeccably. I was surprised to see men wearing suit jackets and women in dresses, and the many school children on the train (clearly heading to the holy shrines) were well dressed, if not in school uniforms, then in something close to it. (I had on camping pants and a backpack, but no one seemed to mind.) The women had their heads covered, as all Iranian women do in public, but no air of religious fanaticism went with the train or the trip. Aside from the headdresses, the crowd moving toward the line of sleepers could well have been boarding the *Twentieth Century Limited* at Grand Central Terminal in the 1960s.

Farshad and I were lucky to have a compartment to ourselves. He went in the upper bunk on one side, and I was in the lower bunk across the aisle so I could look out the window, at least in the morning. We snacked on cookies from the train station (Iranian Oreos) and drank water as the train departed the station. The cars were new and appeared to me to be Chinese-made sleepers—among my favorites on the rails. I had clean, starched sheets and a heavy blanket, and never woke up once during the night, which ended around 6:30 a.m., when I peeled back the curtain and saw a light mist floating over the irrigated farmland that stretched to the horizon.

The train arrived in Mashhad sometime after breakfast, which was a muffin and tea, served in the compartment. We shuffled off the train, took some pictures on the platform ("yes, fine, go ahead"), and got in a taxi for the short ride to the hotel.

The hotel in Mashhad was three stars, neither a dump nor luxurious, but with a friendly staff that would bring me tea any time I sat with my books in the lobby. My room could have slept a family of eight. Murphy beds lined the walls, and cots were in distant corners. I imagined pilgrims in my room, heating food in the microwave oven or drying clothes on the lines that stretched across the bathroom ceiling.

The weather in Mashhad was cold and wet, with a steady drizzle for much of the two days we were there. We walked everywhere, and usually cut through the holy shrine dedicated to the eighth imam, Imam Reza. The city grew up around the tomb, rather than the other way around, and now the shrine covers hundreds of acres in downtown Mashhad, much the way Central Park dominates upper Manhattan, except underfoot in the shrine is marble that grows slick in the rain.

We didn't go once to the shrine, but many times, to this museum or that tomb. Sometimes we just idled in the shrine and talked, or Farshad would check his e-mail on his phone. What I thought would be the center of fundamentalism turned out to be a congregation of believers, some of whom were prostrated in front of the tomb, while others sat around the mosques as might picnickers at a country fair.

After wandering through the shrine—it was especially festive at night—we went off to the tomb of Ferdowsi, a national poet along the lines of Homer, who wrote:

I shall not die, these seeds I've sown will save
My name and reputation from the grave

His tomb sits in a park outside the city, where groups of schoolboys were paying reverence to the departed spirit and tearing around the grounds on go-carts, which were for rent in the parking lot. At the nearby Haruniyeh Dome, a teacher leading a high school group asked me to speak to his students about where I was from, what I had seen in Iran, and where I was going. The boys, all about sixteen, asked questions, shook my hand, stood for pictures with me, and asked for my autograph. (The class was from western Iran, not far from the border with Iraq.) They looked like the boys in my son's classes, and I teased them about missing school.

And, on the way back from Ferdowsi's tomb, we visited the monument for Naser Shah, who founded the Afsharid dynasty (1736–1747), which stretched the borders of Iran from the Caucasus to India. The reign lasted until 1803, and he brought back the Peacock Throne.

Robert Byron's *Road to Oxiana*

BECAUSE IT WAS RAINING AND COLD, I spent a fair amount of time that afternoon back in the hotel, drinking tea and reading Robert Byron's *The Road to Oxiana*. I had bought the book in 1982, when my friend Simon Winchester pronounced it among the best travel books ever written. That year, I read about 100 pages. I can't remember whether I found the writing too British or too obscure (in 1933 Byron went in search of Persian ruins, leaving from Beirut), but I did put it aside. It sat prominently on my shelves, and whenever I would look at it, I felt a vague sense of regret for not being able to finish it. I had no doubt it was great, I just wasn't able keep up with the classical allusions.

When it came time to pack some books for this trip, I made room for Byron. (He was distantly related to the poet.) In the intervening thirty-two years, either Byron had changed, or I had. Just rereading the first hundred pages had me convinced I had made a grave mistake in putting him aside. The writing was fresh, erudite, and amusing. When asked by the Hazrat Sahib, "What government do you belong to?" Byron answers: "The Government of Inglistan."

More pertinent, Byron had gone to all the places I was to see in Iran. In the end, I left behind my guidebook (even in print, I find guide-speak oppressive) and chose Byron as my in-print travel companion. I might miss the best bazaar restaurant, but for the rest of the journey my seat mate would be an eccentric Englishman, who would say things such as: "The noise of the Arabic conversation, punctuated by gurks and gulps, reminded me of Winston Churchill making a speech."

Another reason that I had tracked down Byron in 1982 was because in his history of travel writing, *Abroad*, the essayist Paul Fussell sings his praises: "If we still believed that the souls of the dead could assist and comfort us, he would be venerated as the saint of all whose imaginations come alight at the thought of travel in the now obsolete sense." Fussell also sets the story of Byron's writing, explaining that, before heading east, Byron had washed out of Oxford. Evelyn Waugh said, "he hadn't done his work and was sent down without a degree, so he turned against the classics." One way to read *The Road to Oxiana* is as a revenge against the dons, or as proof, on Byron's eccentric terms, that he was capable of first-class study.

In 1941, two days short of his thirty-sixth birthday, Byron died tragically on a sunk British warship that was bound for the Middle East where he was to take up duties as a war correspondent. Before that, he wrote several books of travel, including accounts of Mount Athos in Greece, and another called *First Russia, Then Tibet*, which has the feel of two books in one. *Oxiana* is the book of his still read today, for its language—at once serious and absurd, but always engaging—and because he reached a part of the world—Iran and Afghanistan—that remain in the back of beyond.

The Road to Oxiana is written in diary form, but Byron did not simply publish his notebooks. Quoting Byron's friend Lord Acton, Fussell explains that Byron "devoted three years to the task, and labored hard 'to obtain an effect of spontaneity.'" The result is a book that is best in its class, as Fussell writes:

> Its distinction tempts one to overpraise, but perhaps it may not be going too far to say that what *Ulysses* is to the novel between the wars and what *The Waste Land* is to poetry, *The Road to Oxiana* is to the travel book. It is virtually unknown in the United States, a fact I take to imply serious cultural impoverishment.

While I am not sure I would elevate it to such company—much as I like the book—I did appreciate having Byron as my narrator, especially as he devotes a considerable portion of the book to Mashhad, where he was determined to gain entrance to the shrine. (In 1933, only believers were admitted.)

He first sets the stage by describing his journey east:

> Century by century, since the Imam Riza was interred beside the Caliph Harun-al-Rashid, this vision has refreshed the desert-weary sight of pilgrims, merchants, armies, kings, and travellers—to become the last hope of several dozen fretful passengers in a damaged motor-bus.

While plotting his way into the shrine, Byron makes a side trip to the tomb of Ferdowsi, writing: "Foreigners have heard of Firdaussi. They esteem him as only a poet can be esteemed whom no one has ever read. And it is expected, therefore, that their tributes will flatter not his work so much as his nationality. Such at least is the Persian hope."

To gain entrance to the Mashhad shrine, Byron dresses up, as only an Englishman can, as if getting ready for a masked ball. He jokes with his traveling companion, Christopher Sykes, that an updated guidebook to Persia should include this sentence: "Visitors intending to inspect the Shrine of the Imam Riza usually dine and make up at the Hotel de Paris."

Once inside Byron writes: "Turbaned mullahs, white-robed Afghans, vanished like ghosts between the orbits of the lamps, gliding across the black pavement to prostrate themselves beneath the golden doorway." I found those same mullahs still at the door, and the women entering the shine wore flowing black capes, as if at a witches' fair, although they moved around with calm purpose.

A museum about the history of the shrine told the story of its recent renovation—well, in the last hundred years—when much of the city was cleared away from the courtyards. Previously, the tomb of Imam Reza was squeezed into the city center, and all around the shrine were the alleys of the bazaar. Now, almost like a Spanish courtyard, the entry to the shrine is a broad concourse of marble, which in the rain felt almost like ice underfoot. On sunny days, especially in spring and fall, the courtyard is filled with pilgrims, waiting for their chance to go inside.

In February, however, the piazza had only small clusters of the faithful. Some huddled under umbrellas, perhaps sharing Byron's fervor. He writes: "I must and will penetrate this mosque before I leave Persia." When Byron went in, it was the equivalent of an infidel's visit to Mecca, one reason the book was such a sensation in the 1930s.

Across the Delta One Desert

LATE IN THE AFTERNOON, Farshad and I boarded an overnight train for Esfahan, which, once Iran is reintegrated into the community of nations, will develop a following similar to that of Florence or Prague (and become equally overrun with tourists).

At first, I was assigned a top bunk in a compartment filled with luggage and children, and an older couple who didn't know what to make of their European traveling companion. Farshad spoke with the conductor, who moved us, together, to another compartment, which we had to ourselves, giving me a lot of room to spread out my map and plot our progress across the center of Iran. Esfahan is an overnight journey, to the south and west of Mashhad, and much of it is across a vast stretch of desert.

During the night, I figured out that we would pass near to Desert One, the name given to the rendezvous place for Delta One on its 1980 mission to free the American hostages. A squadron of eight helicopters flew there in April 1980 (Carter thought the negotiations were going nowhere and, in an election year with a Democratic challenger, he felt he needed to act).

The purpose was to refuel the helicopters at Desert One, and the next night to fly closer to Tehran, where members of the army's elite Delta Force would shift to trucks, drive to the American embassy, shoot their way in, and free the hostages. It was a plan that required the alignment of more stars than are in the Milky Way, and things went bad almost immediately. Three of the eight helicopters broke down for various reasons as they flew into Iran. Then, at Desert One, as the mission was being aborted, one of the helicopters collided with a refueling tanker, which ignited into a fireball that killed eight members of the rescue team. Several helicopters were abandoned in the desert, and the surviving members of the mission withdrew.

The next day, the Carter administration admitted that the operation had been a failure, and the fiasco became synonymous with the ineffectiveness that many Americans perceived about the President. (Clare Boothe Luce said: "The United States will end up apologizing to Iran for it having declared war on us.") It also convinced many Iranians that the United States was an aggressive power, the Great Satan indeed.

Another of the books I had read before the trip was Mark Bowden's *Guests of the Ayatollah*, a long account of the hostage crisis and the aborted rescue. I bought the book in 2006, after it was serialized in the *Atlantic*, and had added it to my Iran book pile, for the day when I might go there.

Bowden describes the ordeal with cinematic detail— recreating the dialogue and scenes of the hostage taking, the negotiations to free them, and the failed rescue attempt. I had found the book an endless magazine story, long on descriptions, short on the reasons why. Nevertheless, when I finished it, I shared Bowden's disbelief that anyone in Washington or the military could have cooked up Operation Eagle Claw as anything other than a video game. (The animated Brzezinski wanted the United States to seize oil-rich Kharg Island and barter that for the hostages. It might not have gotten anyone released, but it for sure would have padded the take on the final accounting of the asset embargo freeze.)

Even if Delta Force had succeeded in getting to the trucks hidden on the outskirts of Tehran, I have my doubts that they could have navigated the city traffic and extracted the hostages without many (both soldiers and hostages) getting killed in the process. Bad as it was that the operation failed at Desert One, the consequences could have been much worse had the Delta One soldiers themselves been taken hostage or killed outside the embassy. It was a plan of endless compromises (so that each branch of the service could have their men involved). At best, the force would have shot their way into the embassy, killing students and guards, until the Iranian police and military overwhelmed them either at the embassy or on the truck ride back out of town to the waiting helicopters.

Bowden covers the story of the "Canadian six" in less than a page, including a quote from an Iranian official who is outraged that Canada had "flagrantly violated international law." Bowden's book would not have been a background source for *Argo*, because in some of its better sections, it describes the extent to which the CIA failed miserably to understand the situation in Iran. He writes:

> A CIA analysis in August 1978, just six months before Pahlavi fled Iran for good, had concluded that the country "is not in a revolutionary or even a prerevolutionary situation."
>
> .... The CIA had not been actively spying in Iran for years. That was part of the problem. It was why no one had ade-

quately foreseen the collapse of the shah's regime. The agency had more or less ceded all intelligence work inside the country to SAVAK, since the shah's enemies tended also to be enemies of the United States.

Even the shredded embassy papers, which students painstakingly reassembled into eighty-five bound volumes of Great Satanism, showed how little the CIA understood of the backstory about the hostages or Iran. (No wonder the CIA opened its doors to Affleck, who in the film can be seen striding purposefully through the agency's actual lobby.) Bowden writes:

> While the zealots did their best to spin conspiracy theories out of the mostly pedestrian cables and memos, the documents utterly exploded the myth of CIA omnipresence and omnipotence. They revealed that the agency's operation in Iran in November 1979 consisted of four Americans (one of the officers had been on home leave when the embassy was taken) who had been desperately knocking on doors and offering cash to anyone willing to help explain to them what was going on. Sheikh-ol-eslam found it incredible that the vaunted CIA had not one officer in his country that could speak Farsi. But the cables confirmed it. Their evil dragon had turned out to be a mouse.

An Art History Class in Esfahan

IT WAS MID-MORNING BEFORE THE TRAIN ARRIVED at the Esfahan station, which is some thirty minutes outside the downtown part of the old city. The parents of the many school children on the train were waiting on the platform with flowers, and as Farshad and I walked to the cab rank, I saw many boys from the sleeping car clutching roses.

The hotel in Esfahan was on the edge of the bazaar and the old city. We left our luggage in the rooms and headed to the bazaar—even quieter than the one in Tehran—and Naqsh-e Jahan Square, which is the vast, open courtyard at Esfahan's cultural center, off of which there are mosques, palaces, and modern city blocks. When Byron stood here in 1933, he wrote:

> At the near end, by me, stands the ruin of the Bazaar Gate; at the far, facing it, the blue portal of the Masjid-i Shah, with dome, ivan, and minarets clumped obliquely behind it, in the direction of Mecca; in front of each, a pair of marble goal posts for polo. On the right rises that brick boot-box the Ali Gapu; opposite, the flowered saucer dome of the Mosque of Sheikh Lutfullah, skewed sideways over a blue recess. Symmetry; but not too much. The beauty lies in the contrast between a formal space and a romantic diversity of buildings.

As best as I could tell, the mosques on the Maidan are no longer working, but operate as historical sites. (Unlike the shrine in Mashhad, which is open for religious business.) Because it was February, we had them to ourselves, and we spent the most time at the Mosque of Sheikh Lutfullah, which is a soaring dome of delicate mosaic design and one of the wonders of the Islamic art world. Byron went there more than once, and not simply to make some of his droll comments. He writes: "In the Mosque of Sheikh Lutfullah, it is a richness of light and surface, of pattern and colour only. The architectural form is unimportant. It is not smothered, as in rococo; it is simply the instrument of a spectacle, as earth is the instrument of a garden."

In moving around Esfahan that afternoon, I spotted a business, run out of a shipping container, that rented bicycles. The next day, we were there when it opened, and we rented two bikes, of the clunker variety, that rattled whenever they rolled over cobblestones, which was all the time. The only ones biking in Tehran, to paraphrase what the humorist S.J. Perelman said about its pedestrians, are "the quick and the dead." Esfahan, however, looked more promising, as it has riverside paths and narrow alleys through the old quarter. After a day on the bike, I cannot say it's the ideal cycling city, although we went everywhere, including into heavy traffic, and had no troubles.

We started riding along the Zayandeh River, which Farshad explained is unusual because it starts in the ground and ends in the ground (not in the sea or another river). The spring rains had yet to begin, so the water level was low, and rocks were visible along both shores. We lingered crossing the Khaju Bridge, which feels Florentine in its execution, with arches across the river and a villa in the center (so that the family of Shah Abbas could enjoy the water views).

Further away from the city we rode to Jolfa, where we peeked briefly into the Vank Cathedral (Bible scenes lined the walls) and then went across the street to a small Armenian museum, which includes the Edict of Shah Abbas in 1618, welcoming Armenians to Persia. (Jolfa is the name of a town, as well, in historic Armenia.)

I took pictures of some paintings (Mount Ararat figures in many) and maps of the diaspora that, after the Turkish genocide, scattered Armenians around the Middle East, especially to Aleppo and Tehran. Some cabinets had books about the genocide, and I found one that I have long wanted to own: *The Treatment of Armenians in the Ottoman Empire*, 1915–1916, by Lord James Bryce and Arnold Toynbee.

From the museum, we biked around the Armenian Quarter, but what struck me most was how assimilated Armenians had become in Iran. From the look of the shops and the restaurant where we ate lunch, what became clear is that most local Armenians cling to their ancient nationality in the way that ethnic Americans might recall, wistfully, that their ancestors came from Poland or Ireland. Yes, they thought of themselves as Armenians and carried on with their Christian churches, but the women wore headscarves and their first language was Farsi.

I never could access the Internet to send messages while in Iran—no one was sure why I was having such trouble, although I suspected the problem lay between Google and the Islamic Republic of Iran. Occasionally I could receive e-mail (which brought me up to date on family news), and that afternoon we stopped in an Internet café (a sorry affair, with two old PCs), which let me check sports scores but proved no more accessible to my e-mail than had my laptop. I seemed the only one who had problems logging onto the Internet. Farshad had total access on his phone, and he even showed me an app, Open Door, that could access sites that the government otherwise had blocked.

Before returning the bikes, we rode to the splendid Jame Mosque, parts of which date to the 11th and 12th centuries. As with the rest of Esfahan, it was largely empty of tourists and travelers. (I can well imagine the crowds after Iran is rediscovered.) We strolled around in solitude, and I was moved to find an antechamber to the mosque that was lined with gothic arches (three centuries before they made their way to Europe). A sign called it the "Gonbad Khaneh" or dome chamber, and the arches here, made of small bricks and mortar, are apparently some of the earliest ever made in the world.

I thought of my college art history course, when gothic arches spoke of the coming Renaissance. Little did Professor James Turnure tell us (in his art history class) that Esfahan's arches were contemporaries of those at the cathedral of Reims or others brought to England during the Norman invasions. Byron found the art and architecture stark, as when he wrote:

> They have art, but not spontaneous art, and certainly not great art. Instead of mind or feeling, they exhale a soulless refinement, a veneer adopted by the Asiatic whose own artistic instinct has been fettered and devitalised by contact with the Mediterranean. To see what that instinct really was, and how it differs from this, one can look at the Assyrian reliefs in the British Museum.

When we finished walking around, we sat in the sun of the courtyard (or *sahn*), a vast empty space of marble paving stones surrounded on all sides by two stories of arches. A sanctuary far removed from civilization? Yes. "Soulless refinement?" Hardly.

Later that afternoon, after returning the bikes, I decided to do most of my shopping in Esfahan, and I happily wandered the bazaar, buying ceramic mugs, delicately engraved metal plates, charms for charm bracelets, and fabric for tablecloths. Nobody shouted at me to close a deal, and I felt under no pressure to buy.

Walking in the bazaar I thought of the near endless nuclear negotiations between Iran and a coalition of Western powers. How many in these talks thought of the Iranians—as did British Foreign Secretary Anthony Eden—as "rug merchants." Yes, they do sell carpets—and exquisite ones at that—but I found their attitude about business and bargaining diffident, to put it mildly.

Several times I stood next to a pile of carpets, running my hands over the woven silk, while in the back of the shop, a group of young men smoked or drank tea, indifferent to the Western tourist in the market. When I did buy some small rugs in Esfahan, the transaction was absent all the histrionics that goes with such a deal in, say, Turkey, where once a carpet dealer was still unfurling his wares in my direction as the taxi I was in drove away.

Vita Sackville-West Travels to Tehran in 1926

THE NEXT DAY WE WERE OFF to the mud city of Yazd, in the desert to the east of Esfahan. I had been told it would be on the train, but the service goes only every other day, and today no train was running. Instead, we took a Ham Safar VIP bus to Yazd, about a four-hour ride across the desert. Alas, VIP is the adjective that modifies all buses in Iran; to be fair to this class of travel, the vehicle was spotless, an attendant passed out water bottles, and my seat was spacious.

What I loved about my travels across Iran, this bus ride included, is that I saw many things, but still had hours each day for reading my books. I read most evenings before going to sleep (we tended to eat early and go back to the hotel), and I read for hours on trains and buses.

Between the books on my Kindle and in my backpack, I was always trying to calibrate my reading to where I was, and on this segment of the journey I read Vita Sackville-West's *Passenger to Tehran*, a 1926 account of her trip east (out through Egypt and Iraq, back through Russia) to visit her husband in Tehran, where he was stationed as a diplomat.

While in Iran, she makes side trips, to Esfahan and, as I discovered, to Yazd, which is more an oasis than a city. On a bus in the middle of nowhere, I was pleased to read her words: "It would seem, however, that Persia is a country made for wandering onward; there is so much room, and no boundaries anywhere, and time is marked only by the sun."

Vita Sackville-West's husband was Harold Nicholson, himself a distinguished historian and writer. Here he remains in the shadows, while on center stage, traveling the world, is his independent and strong-willed wife. While she writes well and gracefully, Vita is remembered in history not for her travel books or her novels but for a string of celebrated love affairs, which included members of both sexes.

Among her lovers was the writer Virginia Woolf, and Vita was a fixture at Bloomsbury. Her son Nigel Nicolson said of his mother: "She fought for the right to love, men and women, rejecting the conventions that marriage demands exclusive love, and that women should love only men, and men only women. For this she was prepared to give up everything..."

Her book about Iran lacks Byron's playfulness and humor, but in Baghdad on the way to Persia, she takes tea with Gertrude Bell in her cottage, writing: "I was only a bird of passage. Next evening I left for Persia, the moon hanging full over Bagdad, and my heart warmed with the anticipation of a return to that friendly little house which now I shall never see again." Bell died a short time later, depriving Britain and the world of her long experience in the Middle East.

Passenger to Tehran is less than 200 pages, and my edition had many black-and-white photographs for illustrations, making it an easy read. Less than half of the book deals with Persia, although when later I was looking back at the passages I had marked, I found that some of her descriptions exactly matched my own conclusions. For example, she writes about Tehran:

Never did any capital look less of a capital, even of Persia, partially, I daresay, because it is dwarfed by the immensity in which it lies; yet in fact it is a great rambling place, with its bazaars that wander for miles, breaking now and then into open lanes between mud-walls, but always creeping again beneath vaulted tunnels, like an animal going into its burrow.

Of the bazaar, Sackville-West writes: "Even the shopkeepers show no anxiety to sell their wares; one may pause and turn over a bundle of silks, or point, admire, and discuss, without hearing the 'Buy! buy!' that assails one in Cairo or Constantinople."

In Esfahan, she admires the Mosque of Sheikh Lutfullah, leaving us an impression even more vivid than that of Byron's (less descriptive, more emotional). She writes: "But by far the most lovely thing I saw in Isfahan, one of those things whose loveliness endures as a melody in the mind, was the Madrasseh, meaning school; but if a school at all, then a school for pensiveness, for contemplation, for spiritual withdrawal; a school in which to learn to be alone." Ten years later, Byron teased her in print: "We seem to be approaching a mediaeval tyranny of modern sensibilities. There was a diplomatic incident when Mrs. Nicolson told the English public she could buy no marmalade in Teheran."

By good fortune, Sackville-West is in Tehran during the installation of Reza Shah, which takes place in the Golestan Palace ("At the top of this staircase was an enormous room, known as the museum, its walls lined with glass cases contained an extraordinary assortment of objects, from Sassanian pottery down to the toothbrushes of Nasred-Din Shah"). When later, in print, she called the new shah a "Cossack trooper... with a brutal jowl," her husband's bosses took Harold aside and asked him to shorten her leash. The full passage reads as follows:

> In appearance Reza was an alarming man, six foot three in height, with a sullen manner, a huge nose, grizzled hair and a brutal jowl; he looked, in fact, what he was, a Cossack trooper; but there was no denying that he had a kingly presence. Looking back, it seemed that he had risen in an amazingly short time from obscurity to his present position; the army was his creation and stood solid behind him.

Her description of Mohammad Reza Shah, as a small boy at his father's coronation, captures what later brought him down in 1979—the petulance of a crown prince. She writes: "The Crown Prince was a dear little boy, was he not, with his miniature sword and his shiny boots? A horrid little boy really, said some one else; he has a violent temper and beats his servants with his fists." He was still beating his servants with his fists when SAVAK was propping up his throne.

Like No Other Persian Town

THE HOTEL ORIENT IN YAZD, a taxi ride from the bus station, was on the edge of the old quarter. When we arrived, there was a problem with the reservation, so I spent a comfortable hour in the expansive lobby, drinking tea and finishing Vita Sackville-West.

Yazd is a city of what look like mud-dwellings. Even the mosques have the look of sandcastles. After lunch (I refused to tip the waiter after he kicked a hovering cat), we wandered through the back alleys, occasionally poking our heads above the ramparts to look at the skyline, which is notable for pre-historic air vents that sit atop many buildings.

These towers look like harmonicas or beehives, and they are to draw cool air into the parlor of an important home. They are everywhere in old Yazd, although I never stood below one to see how much cool air they actually absorb. Byron describes the town:

> Yazd is unlike other Persian towns. No belt of gardens,
> no cool blue domes, defend it from the forbidding
> wastes outside. Town and desert are of one colour, one
> substance; the first grows out of the second, and the tall
> wind-towers, a witness of the heat, are such a forest as a
> desert might grow naturally.

In the late afternoon we took a taxi outside the city to an ancient necropolis and walked up a long hillside, from which the tombs had the look of an ant farm. Back in town we stopped at a Zoroastrian temple built in 1934 (the Nazis copied their eagle symbol), and joined the lines at Haj Khalifeh Rahbar Confectionary, a famous sweet shop from which Iranians from around the country order their cookies and candy (delightful) for the new year holiday.

Early the next morning, after breakfast on a terrace that overlooked the old quarter and its skyline of minarets and mud fans, we were back on the bus, this time to Shiraz.

Ahmadinejad Takes on the World

THE BUS RIDE LASTED ABOUT FOUR HOURS, on a desert highway that was, here and there, lined with factories or industry. I dozed, looked out the window, and read a long analysis of Iran in the world, entitled *Guardians of the Revolution: Iran and the World in the Age of the Ayatollahs* by Ray Takeyh, who is, according to the attached materials, a senior fellow at the Council on Foreign Relations in New York and a former State Department official. He was born in Tehran and has a degree from Oxford University, and his book popped up from a list of books that Amazon thought I might like. (Iran should hire Amazon to track its citizens.)

From Takeyh's writing, I sense he's either a Washington insider or someone who would like to be one. He praises Jimmy Carter for his handling of the hostage crisis (not many do that), explains how Khomeini launched a revolution that wasn't simply Iranian but Islamic ("one of the most successful revolutionary leaders of the twentieth century") and finally many pages later, admits that the ayatollah governed with the autocratic zeal that Stalin might well have understood. (He writes: "In 1988, shortly after the ceasefire with Iraq, the imam ordered one of his last acts of bloodletting. In less than a month, contrived tribunals executed approximately twenty-eight hundred leftist prisoners who were languishing in Iran's jails. Apostasy and the denigration of Islam were the typical charges hurled at the victims.")

In explaining the failures of the Rafsanjani government's reform to bring liberal democratic moderation to the theocratic Islamic state, he writes:

Rafsanjani's economic modernization found political expression in the party known as Karguzaran-i Sazandagi (Servants of Construction), which had been formed by his allies in 1996. The essence of their message was that a strong state was necessary for the creation of a modern, industrial economy capable of generating exports, distributing wealth and services, and providing full employment.... Rafsanjani's government accumulated a debt of approximately $28 billion, a startling figure for a country that went through the war without incurring substantial arrears. In due course, the twin forces of inflation and unemployment would inflict their own damage on Rafsanjani's designs.

In one of the book's better sections, the author describes how Iranian foreign policy since the early 1980s has been its own worst enemy and tone deaf to the issues that drive international consensus. Takeyh writes:

Whether it was plotting a coup in Bahrain, bombings in Kuwait, or instigating riots during the annual Hajj pilgrimages, Iran quickly estranged its neighbors. In a retrospective gaze, Ayatollah Muntaziri, who has grown moderate since being ousted from power, noted Iran's complicity in its fate: "Our harsh slogans against them and talk of exporting the revolution provoked them to act against us and these slogans became the basis for provoking Iraq and causing eight years of war."

Against all norms of international law and politics, the Iranian Government held hostage the diplomats of a sovereign state. Next it embraced terror in the Lebanese civil war by funding car bombs and collecting more hostages. In the mid-1980s, Iran extended the border war into Iraq, turning even the despotic Saddam Hussein into an aggrieved party. It cheered China's massacre in Tiananmen Square and bought weapons from North Korea, later earning a place on George W. Bush's "axis of evil." It organized the bombing of a Jewish cultural center in Buenos Aires and other acts of terror. In the 1990s, 270 Iran legislators signed a petition urging the "annihilation of Israel from the world map" and the government organized a celebration when Israeli Prime Minister Yitzhak Rabin was assassinated. Later, when Mahmoud Ahmadinejad was president, he managed to turn the entire nation into a state of Holocaust deniers.

Despite managing such a portfolio of darkness, Iran still managed, according to Takeyh, "to give birth to one of the most intellectually vibrant democratic movements in the contemporary Middle East." He says that about the government of Muhammad Khatami, who was close to "establishing a novel form of government—an Islamic democracy." He had written books denouncing Marxism ("a satanic ideology") and argued that an Islamic government need not, automatically, recite the satanic verses. Little wonder he failed to convince his overlords on the Guardian Council, as Takeyh writes:

> [A]t its core, a movement that emphasized the need for the public's consent, respect for global opinion, and the relaxation of cultural restrictions was a denial of the imam's politics of intolerance.... Unlike his many counterparts, Khatami was neither corrupt nor a participant in the shadowy violent wing of the Islamic Republic. His

approach to Islam was to emphasize its tolerant side, as he often stressed that religion should not be interpreted to justify dictatorship in the guise of a divine mandate.

Takeyh describes President Mahmoud Ahmadinejad as a professional politician who knew it was in his best interests to sing along with the revolutionary chorus rather than try to improve the lives of his constituents, either when he was mayor of Tehran or president of the republic. Takeyh writes that, as mayor, he "avoided concerted economic planning and relied instead on rash populist measures such as handing out loans to his low-income constituents. While his predecessor focused on building recreational facilities and public parks, he concentrated on refurbishing mosques and religious centers."

Ahmadinejad was meticulous in taking care of his supporters, as most of the city contracts were awarded to members of the Revolutionary Guards and the Basij. His idea of civic improvement was to lay new tracks to the Jamkaran mosque, outside Tehran. ("Beyond a demonstration of his religiosity, this was also smart politics. Many lower- and working-class residents of Tehran believed in the redemptive powers of Jamkaran and thanked the new mayor for providing them a convenient means of reaching their spiritual destination.")

Despite some excellent analysis of Iranian politics, Takeyh ends his book without putting forward any suggestions on how to deal with such an intransigent state. Confrontation? Accommodation? He doesn't say. He warns that the "grand U.S.-Arab alliance to contain Iran is not achievable, will not work, and may make things worse by sinking Iraq, Afghanistan, and Lebanon into greater chaos, inflaming

Islamic radicalism, and further committing the United States to a long and costly presence in the Middle East."

Left aside from the book is that the failure of American policies in Iraq, Afghanistan, Syria, Egypt, Libya, and Lebanon has left Iran as the predominant power in the Middle East. But then, no one gets ahead in Washington by reminding the boss of his errors.

Taking Pictures in Persepolis

AFTER THE RELIGIOUS FERVOR OF MASHHAD and the snow of North Tehran (even Esfahan was chilly at night), Shiraz felt like Florida in springtime. Palm trees lined some of the main streets, the sidewalks were easy for strolling, and the evening air had the scent of jasmine. We went to the central fortress (Karim Khan, which Mohmmad Shah used as a prison), Vakil Mosque (more medieval arches), and the mausoleum of Sayyed Mir Ahmed, the brother of Imam Reza (its golden dome shimmered in the spring air).

Much of what we did in Shiraz was window shop—either in the bazaar or along the boulevards. I bought a map of the Persian Empire, and Farshad talked about the Chinese influence on Iran's market economy, a result of Western sanctions. In general, we talked more about history than politics. I didn't want to make him uncomfortable by discussing political questions, although I think he would have answered anything I asked.

On my last day in Shiraz, Farshad borrowed his family's car and drove me out to Persepolis, which is about an hour northeast of Shiraz. We could easily have hired a taxi, but he thought it would be more comfortable in his father's sedan, which had air conditioning.

Before heading to Persepolis, however, we detoured to Naghsh-e-Rostam, a burial ground for many of the Persian kings, including Darius, Xerxes I, Artaxerxes I, and Darius

II. The tombs were cut high into the hillsides, making them difficult to loot (although they were). I was reminded of similar tombs in Petra, which shares with Naghsh-e-Rostam its rose-red stone.

Under many of the Persian tombs there are reliefs of great scenes from across Persian history (the Investiture of Ardashir I, 224–39 A.D.), although no mention of the Persian Wars that were lost to the Greeks of Athens and Sparta, notably at Thermopylae (the Spartans were told: "Come home with your shield or on it") and the naval battle at Salamis (at which the enraged Persian commander, Xerxes I, shouted: "My men fight like women, and my women fight like men," because it turned out his best officer in the fight [Artemisia I of Caria] was a woman in disguise).

Persepolis is the reason many people either go to Iran or think they want to go to Iran. It was never a city of everyday life, but a showcase, built as Persia's ceremonial capital where envoys could leave offerings, especially during what was known as the "Festival of Tribute." Alexander hated it—the symbol he set out to conquer in the East—and he looted and burned Persepolis in 330 CE. It was also payback for the Persians burning Athens during the Persian Wars.

For many centuries, Persepolis was lost to the world, mostly covered with sand, until the early twentieth century, when explorers to the east heard of its vanished splendors and began digging around the columns. Even in pictures from the 1920s and 30s, it is little more than a few columns in the desert. Archaeologists under the direction of the University of Chicago's Oriental Institute did much excavation work in the 1930s—some members of the Chicago faculty treated Persepolis as an off-campus club. Mohammad Shah continued the restoration, as a way to buff up his international standing, hoping that his allies and enemies might confuse him with Cyrus.

I loved being in Persepolis more than I liked the actual city or how it has been restored. Because he has been there many times, Farshad gave me its history outside the gate and then left me free to wander the ruins, which I did for about two hours. Sometimes I took time out in the shade, drank water, and read from my books; other times I climbed to the necropolis overlooking Persepolis and looked down on the line of columns and the famous grand staircase. I even tracked down the setting, next to Persepolis, for the shah's 1970 extravaganza, which had left behind outlines of the tent village where all the A-list celebrities had stayed (although these tents had modern plumbing and ready access to champagne).

One of the many subtexts in *The Road to Oxiana* (it's a book of delightful diversions) is Byron's determination to get to Persepolis, which he would have studied at Oxford, and to take pictures of the ruins. ("The start of a journey in Persia resembles an algebraical equation: it may or may not come out.") Opposing him in this endeavor is Dr. Ernst Herzfeld, who works for the University of Chicago as the lead archaeologist in Persepolis. He hates the idea of Byron coming to the site and taking pictures, and denies him authorization to come with a camera. (Today, everyone walks around behind an iPhone.)

The letter to Byron, in part, reads as follows:

For, as soon as a foreigner is seen taking photos, there appear articles in the press (already 3 times) complaining, that everyone is allowed to photograph the National Monuments of Persia except the Persians. I have had the most unpleasant correspondence with the Government on this account.

Yours very sincerely ERNST HERZFELD.

In his letters to friends and his readers, Byron complains that "the German Professor Ernst Herzfeld, in charge of the excavations, has turned Persepolis into his private domain and forbids all picturetaking." Byron decides to ignore him, setting up a comical confrontation between the carefree, eccentric British traveler and the German archaeologist. Byron recounts:

> While I was photographing, a small round figure twinkled across the platform. "I have never," it said, "met with a way of acting as illoyal as yours," pirouetted, and twinkled away again. Illoyal to whom, I wondered. It was a question of principle. I got my pictures, and did a service to travelers in calling Herzfeld's bluff.

Herzfeld later complains about Byron to the University of Chicago, but by then the Englishman is long gone, although not before remarking how different Herzfeld's Persepolis looks from that of Darius I. He writes:

> There are still things to be said about Persepolis. In its prime, when the walls were mud and the roofs wood, it may have looked rather shoddy—rather as it would look, in fact, if reconstructed at Hollywood. Today, at least it is not shoddy. Only the stone has survived, but for a few of Alexander's ashes which they dig up now and then. And stone worked with such opulence and precision has great splendour, whatever one may think of the forms employed on it.

The Shah Dines in the Desert

EQUALLY WORTHY OF BYRON'S PEN was Mohammad Reza Shah's 1970 sound-and-light show in Persepolis to celebrate 2,500 years of the Persian Empire. It was pretty much an update on the Festival of Tribute, except these world leaders, for their gifts, arrived with weapons contracts for the shah.

In his biography of the shah, William Shawcross has long descriptions of the celebration and the logistics required to create a modern banquet hall and tent city in the hot desert. He writes: "The whole affair cost anything up to $300 million (estimates differ) and that in a country where per capita income, though rising, was still only about $500 a year. Moreover, the event seemed to be much more a paean to the Pahlavi family than to Iran."

Nor did the event that catered to the world's celebrity elite involve the Iranian people in the celebration. They could watch on television as the shah greeted his guests in the tents, arranged the dinner parties ("the only food on the menu that was Iranian was the caviar; almost everything else came from France"), or saluted a parade of Persian vassals, in Hollywood costumes, that marched past his reviewing stand. Shawcross quotes one guest: "It was as if some Technicolor epic of Cecil B. DeMille's was being projected on to the screen of the vast plain."

I had another account of the festivities from my friend Eugene Schulman, who gave me a book, *Celebration at*

Persepolis, that the photographer Jacques Lowe (famous for his pictures of the Kennedy family) published in 1971. Eugene was friends with Lowe, who gave him a signed copy. Lowe and a team of photographers had access to the celebration; in retrospect, the shah might have been advised—for the future of his reign—to have adopted Herzfeld's no picture policies.

The book begins with some general shots around Iran—modern Tehran and classical Esfahan—and focuses on the three days in the Persepolis desert. One picture shows the shah with a line of his be-ribboned generals (the same ones who deserted him in 1978), and the photographs of the shah and his wife are captioned: "Their Imperial Majesties."

To the shah's disappointment, the great powers—the United States, Britain, and Russia—snubbed the occasion by not sending their heads of state (Queen Elizabeth, President Nixon, and General Secretary Brezhnev). Instead the shah is shown putting on a happy face while greeting the Russian President Nikolai Podgorny, Vice President Spiro Agnew, and the Queen's daughter, Princess Anne. Imelda Marcos is there—no doubt with suitable shoes for the occasion—and Marshal Tito has the look of an Austro-Hungarian cavalry officer. Lowe has some close-ups of the banquet tables ("Feast of the Century" with quail eggs and, appropriately, stuffed peacock).

Clearly a B-lister, Agnew is shown eating on the first night with some Hollywood actresses, and the next night he is shuffled off to King Hussein's table while the shah sits with the non-aligned nations (safer in 1970 than choosing between the United States and Russia).

The narrow-focused pictures of the great parade, before the walls of Persepolis, give it the air of *Ben-Hur*. All that remains of the pageant are the metal frames of the guests' tents and the line from Christopher Marlow's 1587–88 play, *Tamburlaine the Great, Part I* (which Shawcross quotes): "Is it not fine to be a King and ride in triumph in Persepolis?" The next millennium of the Persian Empire, however, lasted only eight years.

Allah's Disney World

I WAS DUE TO FLY OUT THAT NIGHT to Tehran and wait for my connecting flights to Kiev and Geneva. As we had time, Farshad and I ate lunch in a modern cafeteria (it had air conditioning) and strolled through the elegant Eram Gardens, close to Shiraz University. All the time that we were walking and eating, Farshad was trying to make the most of my last night in Tehran. I would have almost eight hours between the time the Shiraz flight landed at Mehrabad Airport and my next flight left from Imam Khomeini Airport. Maybe, he suggested, I would like to go to Qom, the holy city, which is fairly close to the international airport?

I knew Qom only as the city of Ayatollah Khomeini, and I associated it with clerical fanaticism. I would not have been surprised if the city was closed to foreigners, as is Pyongyang. Most political articles about Iranian politics speak of "hard-liners" in Qom opposing liberal reformists in Tehran, so in my mind the city was off-limits to tourists and reserved for the faithful who went to cheer the Supreme Leader or perhaps work themselves into fits of devotion.

Farshad laughed at my suppositions and said I would enjoy seeing it. The problem was to find a car and driver at the last minute who could meet me in Tehran, take me to Qom, and then drop me off at the international airport. He made several calls, and finally came up with someone willing to do the run for $60. I agreed, and Farshad and I said our good-byes at the Shiraz Airport, where I stood in a long line for the commuter flight (the airplane was a McDonnell-Douglas DC-9) to Tehran. (In articles about economic sanctions, much is made of the fact that local airlines cannot buy spare parts for their American-made planes.) Nevertheless, the plane flew smoothly, without turning once, from Shiraz to Tehran, and I was waiting for my ride by 7:30 that evening.

The first indication that my last-minute driver lacked some essential skills of the driving trade came when we walked to the parking lot and he could not find his car. I followed him around until we agreed that I would wait by the exit while he tracked down the missing car, which took about thirty minutes. Next, he asked if maybe we could drive back into Tehran and pick up his wife? He said she loved Qom and wanted to join us. I eagerly agreed, as I thought maybe his wife could help with directions, and having her in the car might spare me from some of our conversation (which since the airport had focused on his secret habit of smoking cigarettes, which he hid from his wife).

Their apartment building was in central Tehran, although to drive there took some maneuvering through rush-hour traffic. It was a Friday night (a day off) and the elevated highways around Tehran were clogged with cars and mini vans. If my driver was thirty years old, his wife must have been twenty-five, and she worked as a primary school teacher in the neighborhood. Her father had been a senior official with the Iranian railways, and she enjoyed hearing my stories of the overnight train to Mashhad and Esfahan, which she remembered from her childhood.

Very openly, I thought, for an Iranian woman meeting a stranger in her husband's car, she told me she wanted children, but that he was against it. And they both talked at length, as we inched through traffic toward the Qom highway, about their summer plans to join a pilgrimage to Najaf. Aside from her parents, religion was the most important thing in her life, she said, and her dream was to see the holy shrines at Najaf and Karbala. Just that day she had been working on the travel plans, which involved a flight to southern Iraq (away from the violence) and a charter bus ride to Najaf. (I remembered, but said nothing about, Khomeini's flight into Iraqi exile with his son, when no one met them at the airport, and the imam haggled with the cab driver about the fare.)

How this couple had ever come together mystified me. She was elegant, well-spoken, smart, caring, and humorous. He was morose, a terrible driver, and a closet smoker. We pushed on through the night (by now, after the traffic and stops it was close to midnight) until the highway signs indicated exits for Qom.

Sackville-West has a description of Qom's "great gold mosque gleaming brilliant above a field of young wheat," but now it is a pilgrim city with monorails, above-ground parking lots, motels, and food courts. There were even Christmas lights (well, so to speak) along the road as we drove to the main entrance. I had thought I was going into the dragon's den. Instead, I arrived at Allah's Disney World.

We followed the directions of some traffic policemen and parked the car near the shrine in an underground lot. (It felt like we were going to a baseball game.) Kindly, I thought, the driver's wife—to thank me for the trip to Qom—had brought along a picnic supper, and at midnight, as we sat in the parked car, she served chicken and rice, and handed around cans of carbonated soda (not Fanta, but something like it).

It had been ten hours since my last meal, so I was happy to have her grilled chicken and rice (we ate on paper plates, as if it were July 4th), and I told them stories about my children and where they had gone to school. Then we put away the picnic utensils and took an elevator upstairs to the Qom courtyard, from where it was a short walk to the holy shrine.

It felt a little like Vatican City, except that it was much more festive. Small boys were playing tag around the courtyards, and in one corner there was a group of teenage boys, singing songs. They might well have been cruising the Jersey Shore, except above their heads were two large banners showing the portraits of ayatollahs Khomeini and Khamenei, as if on a beachfront billboard. (Looking for Eternity? Why not give us a call at 1-800-SUPREME-LEADER?)

As we entered the second courtyard, in front of the shrine, the husband and wife explained that she was heading for the women's entrance, and he would be praying somewhere else (actually, he whispered to me, he was off to smoke cigarettes). That meant I was on my own in the shrine, and we agreed to meet in an hour. They said I would be fine.

As Farshad and I had been to many mosques, I knew the drill about removing my shoes and carrying them around in a plastic bag. I also knew that I could happily spend the hour watching the faithful go through their prayers and chanting, and if I tired of that, I could always find a quiet corner and read a book on my Kindle.

I didn't stay all that long inside the shrine. Even at midnight, it was busy with pilgrims, but such is the lighting, inside and out, that the setting glowed like an amusement park. I sat inside for a while, took a picture of a mullah checking his cell phone (maybe there is an app for martyrdom?), and drifted outside to the souvenir stands, where I looked at the beads and key chains and waited for the driver and his wife to return.

My outbound flight was at 3:20 a.m., and around 1 a.m. I began to get nervous that the driver might mess up the departure as he had my arrival. They showed up a few minutes later and, in about 40 minutes, were dropping me at the departure level of Imam Khomeini International Airport. I paid the driver, thanked his wife for the dinner, left them my last bar of Swiss chocolate, and joined the scrum at security, which, to my confusion, segregated the luggage of men and women.

There were no scenes like those in *Argo* (when the Revolutionary Guards figure out that the six leaving are U.S. diplomats and probably spies). Instead, the only drama at the airport involved finding someone who might be kind enough to mail my locally stamped postcards. (A duty-free clerk agreed to drop them in a box, and they arrived about three months later.)

Last Night in Tehran

To read on the way home, I chose Reza Kahlili's *A Time to Betray*, which is an autobiographical account of a boy coming of age during the late years of the shah's rule. His parents are wealthy, and his friends are ambitious for Western lives. He attends college at the University of Southern California, but he gets caught up in the Revolution and joins the Revolutionary Guard, where not even the imprisonment and execution of his close childhood friends can break his fervor. He travels to the front of the Iran-Iraq War and remains in revolutionary thrall until he makes a trip back to the United States and offers himself up as a CIA mole in revolutionary Iran. Late in the confessional story he tells his CIA handler: "Carol, it's very important to understand this mentality of martyrdom and radical conviction. They truly believe that one day Islam will conquer the world. If we allow the Guards to go unchecked, the consequences could be devastating for the region—and the world."

Reza Kahlili is a pseudonym. The real name of the author was lost when he defected to the United States— at the end of his time in Iran for the CIA. So no one can know for sure if all aspects of his first-personal story are true. Assuming that many are, his narrative tells a compelling story about the fanaticism in post-Revolutionary Iran, in which Khomeini ran a police state no less savage than that of the shah, and filled up the same prisons with opposition figures.

Of the Revolution's early days, Kahlili writes:

> Every faction and ideology—religious, liberal, secularist, Marxist, or Communist—had rallied under Khomeini's banner. Within a couple of months, the provisional government held a national referendum. The question: Islamic Republic, yes or no? The lack of other options caused some to raise their eyebrows, but in the heady aftermath of Khomeini's return, 98 percent voted yes.

Later, the movement began to devour its own, including many Kahlili had known growing up. He writes:

> At the same time, Hezbollah (Party of God) gangs of radical Islamists, sporting uniforms of dirty long beards and buttoned-up shirts, roamed the streets on motorcycles, brandishing sticks and chains, shouting "Allaho Akbar" and "Khomeini Rahbar" ("Khomeini is our leader"), and attacking people who did not adhere strictly to Islamic rules.... We were caught up in three wars: Iraq against Iran, the Mujahedin against the mullahs, and Hezbollah against the people. Our youth were slaughtered on battlefields and our citizens were rounded up, whipped, beaten, and humiliated as punishment for disobeying some arbitrary rule of decorum.

On another level, *A Time to Betray* is the story of three boys—Reza, Kazem, and Naser—growing up best friends and coming of age during the Revolution. The poorest of the three boys, Kazem embraces revolutionary ideology and joins the

Guards, into which he draws Reza (for a while). Naser wants little to do with revolutionary politics, although through his sister he is drawn into the opposition and later executed by the likes of Kazem. (These passages are the most heart-rending in the book.) Their stories might well describe the divisions that remain in Iranian society.

Reza writes of his upper middle-class childhood in prosperous Tehran:

> Some Muslims, like Kazem's family, held the mullahs in high regard and followed their teachings closely. However, most people—my family and Naser's family among them—considered the mullahs nothing more than low-level preachers who helped them practice their faith and meet their moral obligations. Grandpa did not like the mullahs. I once heard him say, "These donkey riders should all be moved to the city of Qom, where they learned all this nonsense. They should be kept in a compound and only allowed to preach there." And then in a moment of terrible prescience, he added, "God forbid if they ever get the power to rule."

While in the service of the Revolutionary Guards, Kahlili is told that the attack on the U.S. embassy was planned at the highest levels. ("Smiling at me with his candle throwing a beatific glow on his face, Kazem told me that the whole takeover had been planned ahead of time with Khomeini's secret approval. The leaders of the invasion had even dubbed the embassy 'the den of spies' for the media.") Later he verifies that Iran was behind the 1983 Lebanon bombing of a U.S. Marine Corps barracks near Beirut Airport. He says:

Four years after this suicide bombing, Iran's then-minister of the Revolutionary Guards, Mohsen Rafiqdoost, boasted that "Both the TNT and the ideology which in one blast sent to hell four hundred officers, NCOs, and soldiers at the Marines headquarters were provided by Iran."

And he describes how, even into the modern era, the clerics in Qom have managed to keep a stranglehold on Iranian politics. While Iran democratically elects its president, parliament, and municipal officials (unlike many other countries in the Middle East), the mullahs remain in control through the Supreme Leader (who can dissolve any government) and through a guardian council that must ratify all public decisions. (On paper, Britain has a similar system of government, except neither the monarchy nor the House of Lords have any political power.) Kahlili describes the mullah system this way:

...the Guardian Council decided which candidates could run for office and the Council consisted of six members chosen directly by the Supreme Leader, Imam Khomeini, and six more approved by him after their nomination by the chief justice, who was also handpicked by the Supreme Leader, and their election by the parliament. This meant that no one could attain power if they posed even the slightest risk to the status quo.

Caught between many worlds—those of his family and revolutionary Iran, or the struggle between the mullahs and the United States—Kahlili decides that the only way he can rebel against the clerical dictatorship is to spy for the United

States. He confesses: "In spite of their assurances, I felt like a vulnerable child seeking shelter and security. I'd hoped Carol would have better ideas about what to do in my situation, but her only solution was for me to dive back into the world I longed to leave. Again, I felt I had no choice but to comply. I was leading two lives, but neither of them was my own."

Did it work? At the end he writes: "The information I provided to America might have been useful, but it didn't accomplish what I had hoped."

Imperial Persia

THE FLIGHTS HOME TOOK LONGER than the schedule allowed. The connection in Kiev was delayed, and the crowds at airport security took an hour to navigate. As well, from the spring air in Shiraz, I came home to the damp March wind and rain of central Europe.

Back home, what did I think about Iran? I was under no illusion that I had seen much more of the country than tourist Iran (the bridges of Esfahan, the columns at Persepolis). Nevertheless, I never felt threatened or endangered, and I appreciated the clean, modern trains, and the fact that while there—via Whispernet at Amazon—I was free to read any book of my choosing, no matter how damning its message about the Islamic Republic. That said, I saw almost no police on the street and very few soldiers, except at the Iraq-Iran war museum.

I liked Tehran more than I had expected to, and I am glad to have seen Esfahan and Yazd before they are overrun with tourists. (I was reminded of visiting Dubrovnik at the end of the Yugoslav wars, when it was a ghost town, and afterwards, when it was a stop in the cruise ship Magic Kingdom.) I was pleased to have found Robert Byron as one of my traveling companions, and even on the plane home I enjoyed flipping through his diary entries and reading them randomly. (When he and Christopher stop to visit a cave and take some pictures, Byron writes that "Christopher overheard the Chief of Police whisper to the Military Commandant: 'I wonder why the British Government wants photographs of this cave.'") I liked the food and especially the cheerful disposition of my guide, Farshad, to whom I promised to send a copy of *Oxiana*, which he will love.

I largely avoided political conversations. Occasionally, at chance meetings with other travelers, I found myself talking about Iran's nuclear options or the forty-year war with the United States. In that regard, the best idea I heard against giving Iran nuclear capability is that, instead, it should be made the poster child for solar energy. Vast stretches of now empty desert get endless amounts of sun and would be an ideal location for solar panels. What better way to boost the American solar industry than to conclude a long-term deal with Iran, if it needs additional (non-nuclear) power? The only reason Iran clung to its nuclear options, I was told, was because it was in the Iranian nature to hang on to something that someone else wanted. Who knows, maybe they could trade it for something useful? (I can imagine some official thinking: "I wonder why the United States wants photographs of these caves?")

I was surprised at how few people asked me about the United States. Americans, especially American presidents, are preoccupied with Iran, but the reverse is not true, and in two weeks I never heard the names Clinton, Obama, Kerry, Romney, Trump, or Biden. Nobody mentioned them, and no one seemed to care what they thought. On the other hand, Saudi Arabia remains an Iranian obsession—hence the conflict in Yemen—and would seem to drive its foreign policy much more than even Israel or the United States.

I got the feeling that religious Iran was in decline. Yes, the clerics held sway over representative government, and Iran still had its Supreme Leader. But during the day, when the call to prayer would sound at the bazaar or in the metro, no one batted an eye in the direction of Mecca. Nor did I see many young people around the shrines. Those who were there tended to be extended families on a pilgrimage, and as much on a holiday as on a religious quest. Why else would Qom have so many souvenirs for sale?

I liked all the children that I met in my travels. In general, they were well-dressed, polite, and seemed to respect their teachers. I stood with them for pictures all across Iran, talked to them about their classes and school trips, and listened to them tell me about their favorite soccer players. Their school uniforms reminded me more of English boarding schools than of the students who took over the U.S. "Den of Espionage," and the kids I met looked as though they hoped to grow up to be doctors and lawyers, not revolutionaries.

I was surprised at how casual I found the Shia religion. Before, I associated it only with fanatics of the burning-at-the-stake kind or those who filled the streets in a frenzy during Khomeini's funeral and chipped away at his burial gown. Instead, the Shiism on the ground in Iran struck me as much less intense than, say, the Sunnis in Cairo, for whom the call to prayer sounds like a military command. To be sure, many Iranians are devout, and nearly all are Shia, but I wonder if the United States or Iran has more fundamentalists.

Although no one I met wants a royal restoration, a number of people I came across spoke well of the Pahlavis in terms of their infrastructure advancements. Reza Shah built the train line from the Persian Gulf to the Russian border, and Mohammad Shah laid down the highways, extended the power grid, and built many of the airports. He also developed the state university system and encouraged women to attend. The mullahs had said a lot of prayers, but not done much as "river and harbor" men (a phrase from the nineteenth century for politicians who developed infrastructure).

A tragedy of modern Iran is its dependence on the automobile. Iranians drive everywhere, as gasoline is $0.30 a gallon. Gridlock is a problem not just in Tehran (which otherwise would be ideal for bicycles, buses, and pedestrians), but in Esfahan and Mashhad at certain times of the day. I loved the trains, but the only people who take them are school groups, apparently. I met a few Iranians close to my age who said they had not been on a train in decades. Intercity public transportation usually means either flying or VIP buses, but geographically Iran is similar to China, and could easily develop a high-speed rail network. It would be a better investment than nuclear weapons.

Although I didn't get to the north and west of the country, I sensed that Kurdish politics could well dominate the Middle East in future years, almost more than the Arab-Israeli conflict. With all the breakdowns in the central Iraqi state, Kurds in Iraq have been operating autonomously, which has encouraged separatism in Iran and Turkey, two countries that agree on little except the suppression of the Kurds. An independent Kurdistan could find itself at war with Turkey and Iran, although neither power would assist the other in subduing the revolt.

Iran, I inferred, has a lot to lose in the endless Syrian civil wars, especially if Bashir al-Assad (their man in Damascus) is overthrown, which would cut off the aid that Syria (from Iran) sends to Hezbollah in southern Lebanon. (Russia supports Assad but not Iran.) Even in a fragmented condition, the Islamic State (ISIS) is another continuing threat to Assad in Syria and Hezbollah in Lebanon, which is one reason that coalition forces in northern Iraq got support from Iran. To the Iranians, ISIS sounds like a Saudi front organization, and Iran pushes back against Wahhabism whenever it senses its encroachment in Yemen, Bahrain, or in other Gulf states. (The conflict in Yemen is best understood as a proxy war between Iran and Saudi Arabia.) Were Iran not pledged to Israel's destruction (or in a hot-and-cold war with the United States since 1979), the three countries together might find a lot of common security interests, save for Hezbollah on Israel's northern frontier.

When on the ground in Iran, I could make no sense of the nuclear argument between Iran and the United States. (Many tour buses, apparently, roll past the nuclear facility in Natanz, that which Israel has routinely attacked, although I wasn't anywhere near to it.) On paper, anyway, the dispute revolves around whether Iran has ambitions for a nuclear weapon (I am sure it does) and whether the United States should have allowed it to maintain uranium enrichment facilities (for so-called peaceful purposes). As best as I could tell, Iran needs neither nuclear power plants nor atomic weapons, but as I read the agreement, it got options for both in 2015, plus a lifting of the economic sanctions—on the condition that it ceased threatening Israel, cooperated in going after ISIS, and toned down its nuclear-independence rhetoric. The German word for these treaty expectations is *Zukunftsmusik* or "future music," and the agreement only lasted, in effect, for less than three years. President Trump withdrew American participation from the Joint Comprehensive Plan of Action (JCPOA), on an executive basis, in 2018. After that, his administration took a hard line against Iran, killing the Iranian commander Qassim Suleimani in a drone strike, and supporting Israel's attacks (cyber and otherwise) on Iran's nuclear capabilities, including the assassination of nuclear scientist Mohsen Fakhrizadeh.

When the JCPOA deal was agreed in 2015, the Obama administration gave up everything for some feel-good headlines, and the Iranians got rid of the sanctions and kept their nuclear infrastructure, in exchange for some International Atomic Energy Association inspections. I am not sure what that meant, given than Iran had already signed the Nuclear Non-proliferation Agreement (which provided for inspections). Perhaps Ben Affleck can clear up the confusion in post-production? It worked before, and turned the 1979 hostage crisis from a defeat into a victory, although *Argo* came out too late to help Jimmy Carter win reelection, and the Iranian agreement was a drag on the presidential candidacy of Hillary Clinton in 2016. Saber-rattling Iran, however, did wonders for Donald Trump's presidency, giving him "a good, safe menace" to hold over the American electorate. (Both he and the Iranians loved living in 1979—when one danced to disco and the other to evening prayers.) And I do wonder if the presidency of Joseph R. Biden Jr. will have any luck putting the genie back in the bottle and then locking it away in some cave.

Maybe the better advice came from Robert Byron, who wrote of Reza Pahlavi (Vita Sackville-West's "Cossack trooper" who became the shah of shahs in 1925): "Persia had always been like this. The only thing to do was to have patience till the tyrant died."